Wondrous Wisdom

EVERYONE'S GUIDE
TO AUTHENTIC KABBALAH

By Michael R. Kellogg

Wondrous Wisdom

EVERYONE'S GUIDE
TO AUTHENTIC KABBALAH

UPPER LIGHT
PUBLISHING

By Michael R. Kellogg

Editor: Claire Gerus
Proofreading: Chaim Ratz
Layout: Baruch Khovov

THE WONDROUS WISDOM
OF KABBALAH

EVERYONE'S GUIDE

TO AUTHENTIC KABBALAH

Copyright © 2006 by MICHAEL R. KELLOGG

ISBN: 0-9738268-1-9

FIRST EDITION: FEBRUARY 2006

Dedication

*This book is dedicated to every person
with a point in the heart*

ACKNOWLEDGEMENTS

First, my sincerest thanks to my group of Kabbalah students and friends in St. Louis, Missouri, who gave up many Sunday afternoons in order to help edit this book. There is simply no way to express my gratitude to these wonderful people: JoAnn Adams, Dee Berman, Marlene Bricker, Maureen Burton, Fran Ebel, Judy Hobart, Sally Hori, Ed Magraw, Pam Magraw, Gina Mason, Jim McClaren, David Monolo, Joyce Reese, and Roger Zemen.

To my dear friend, Chaim Ratz, who spent a great deal of time editing and verifying the accuracy of this work's content according to the strict standards of the Kabbalah group, Bnei Baruch in Tel Aviv, Israel. This book would have been totally impossible without your efforts. To Tony Kosinec and Igal Zahavi, my dear friends in the Toronto Bnei Baruch group, who supported me through the entire effort, and usually several times a day!

To my editor, Claire Gerus, I offer my deepest gratitude for her highly professional hard work in editing the book. Thanks to Uri Laitman, who managed the distribution of the book. And a special thanks to my wife, Shari, who was so understanding on those countless nights of late work at the office to complete this work. To my world group, the entire *haverim*, I thank you all for your wonderful thoughts of encouragement and strong intent.

Finally, to my Rav, Kabbalist Michael Laitman, PhD. It is impossible to put into words how fortunate I feel to have a teacher so dedicated to the spiritual growth of his students. Our initial personal relationship began, of all places, in a hotel lobby, where for several hours I peppered Dr. Laitman with questions regarding this wondrous wisdom. He patiently answered every single question, and in so doing, began a relationship that has now spanned years of classes, discussions, meetings, complaints, e-mails, and study, all of which promptly challenged me to delve deeper and deeper ever since.

The author, Mike Kellogg
can be contacted at
mkellogg@upperlightpub.com

Wondrous Wisdom

EVERYONE'S GUIDE TO AUTHENTIC KABBALAH

TABLE OF CONTENTS

INTRODUCTION

Throughout the history of societal development, countless scientific discoveries have been made by men and women seeking solutions to a wide array of problems. Through experimentation, combined with a keen sense of curiosity, human beings have brought great benefits to their world from these discoveries, and the process is actually accelerating.

But what really is a discovery? It is not actually the creation of anything new; it is simply finding what is already there, even if that is a basic concept or idea. Historic inventions that have revolutionized our lives such as the Guttenberg press, the steam engine, and the computer were culminations of ideas already present and waiting to be acted upon. In other words, all great innovations, whether considered inventions or concepts, are like the last link in a series of links in a chain.

A TV program called "Connections" publicized the interconnection between what most people considered a unique event, and that event's origins. The narrator led viewers through a series of events that, by the end of the program, were woven together to produce a final result, usually a major invention of some kind.

The origins, or roots of any subject are of great importance, and as a student of Kabbalah, I feel a deep responsibility to convey where the information contained in this book originated. Like everything that has ever been discovered, the roots of my discovery of Kabbalah do not lie in the words of a book, or from attaining some brilliant independent insight. Rather, my discoveries have been a process of regaining ancient information, provided by Kabbalistic writers who, for centuries, have transmitted this wondrous wisdom to all mankind.

Within the depths of each and every one of us lies a question. It concerns the very nature of our existence, and is usually preceded by a cavalcade of preliminary questions. This question remains dormant until a given moment, one that no one can predict. But when this question evolves

11

to the point where it demands an answer, the response is always supplied through the help of an "end supplier" of that knowledge—a teacher.

My teacher, Kabbalist Rav Michael Laitman, PhD, is the author of twenty-three books on the subject of Kabbalah. His books are currently published in nine languages. I can only convey how this wondrous wisdom is transferred from teacher to student by dedicating a few pages of this introduction to Dr. Laitman's story, as well as to those who were responsible for passing this book on to him.

Dr. Laitman's journey into the wisdom of Kabbalah began like every other individual's spiritual journey, with that same burning question deep within: "Why do I exist?" And like all of us, Dr. Laitman's question was originally ignored or pushed aside by his efforts to lead a normal, comfortable life pursuing educational and business interests.

After immigrating to Israel in 1974, Dr. Laitman, a bio-cyberneticist by profession, led a reasonably normal life with the usual pursuits and hardships experienced by many Israelis in the 1970's. Yet that burning question still came back to haunt him over and over again. One day in 1975 Dr. Laitman chose to attend a lecture on Kabbalah.

Afterwards, feeling a strong attraction to the Wisdom, Dr. Laitman sought a teacher. Yet even though he began lessons with several instructors, most early efforts were discontinued, as he could not find a teacher who would provide satisfactory answers to his questions. As he wrote in his book, *Attaining the Worlds Beyond*, "I began to search for real teachers. I looked through the entire country and took many lessons. But somehow, an inner voice kept telling me that all I came across was not the real Kabbalah, because it did not speak of me, but some distant abstract issues."

In 1979, through a remarkable course of events that lead him to ask a total stranger where he might find instruction in Kabbalah, Dr. Laitman was directed to the man who would become his teacher and mentor, Rav Baruch Ashlag. His initial classes, held between 3:00 a.m. and 6:00 a.m., began with one of the instructors reading an article, Introduction to The Book of *Zohar*. The instructor would read a paragraph, then explain what that paragraph meant. And so Dr. Laitman's initial studies began.

One day, months after beginning his lessons, Dr. Laitman was asked if he could drive the main elder of his study group to see a doctor in Tel Aviv. That main elder was Rav Baruch Ashlag, son of the great Kabbalist, Rav Yehuda Ashlag. During this drive and on subsequent drives to the doctor, Rav Ashlag began instructing Dr. Laitman in Kabbalah. Even when Baruch Ashlag was eventually put in the hospital, Dr. Laitman would go to the hospital at 4:00 a.m. and study with him there. What felt like a rather precarious beginning became a strong relationship between Kabbalist and student that would last for the next twelve years.

The following two excerpts describe his teacher as well as his teacher's teacher.

Rav Baruch Ashlag – Rabash – (1907-1991)

Rav Baruch Ashlag was the next phase in the evolution of Kabbalah after his father, Rav Yehuda Ashlag. Baruch Ashlag was the eldest son of Yehuda Ashlag. Born in Poland in 1907, he came with his father to Israel at the age of 15. He always worked simple jobs: construction worker, road works, a shoemaker, or a clerk. He was never ashamed to do such menial tasks, treating them as a necessity for survival in this world. He was offered quite a few high offices, but never accepted any of them.

He was very knowledgeable in Torah and Talmud, but he never served as a rabbi. Instead, he spent his entire life following in the footsteps of his father and advancing in the study of Kabbalah. When his father passed away, Baruch Ashlag took his place and accepted his father's disciples, continuing his work by publishing *The Zohar* with his father's commentaries, as well as writing several other books.

I had already been in search of a teacher for four years when I came to Rav Baruch Ashlag in 1979. I was studying by myself and with a variety of "Kabbalists." I went a long way knowing I needed to study Kabbalah,

13

but not knowing who could teach me. I knew this was the place for me from the first lesson with Rav Ashlag. I remained with him for twelve years, until his death. When he died I was there at his bedside.

Rav Baruch Ashlag followed in the footsteps of his father. He wrote five books of articles, called *Shlavey HaSulam* (*The Rungs of the Ladder*), where he successfully expressed all the inner situations of a person who is on the way for the attainment of the Upper World. He studied every possible situation, every step and movement that we make on the way, explained the exodus to the spiritual world, and how to feel and live in it.

He constructed a system for the attainment of the Upper World for the individual, something that previous Kabbalists did not do. The uniqueness of his articles is especially significant for those who want to attain the spiritual world. Without these, it is impossible to even imagine an exit to the spiritual world.

He also left us a manuscript of sermons he had heard from his father, which he called *Shamati* (*I Heard*). Using these articles, one can define one's situation, its characteristics and how to continue the spiritual ascent in that situation. The book is the basis for all the situations in the spiritual worlds and their many combinations, all of which can affect the soul of one who aspires to attain them.

The works of Rav Baruch Ashlag are essential to anyone who wishes to open to the spiritual world. After the death of Rav Ashlag, a group was established carrying his name - Bnei Baruch (The Sons of Baruch) - that continues to study in his steps.

Rav Baruch Ashlag obtained this great wisdom through his father, Yehuda Ashlag, also known as Baal HaSulam. The following excerpt from Interview with the Future provides information on this great Kabbalist.

Rav Yehuda Ashlag, Baal HaSulam (1885-1954)

Neither *The Zohar*, nor the writings of the Ari were intended for a systematic study of the Kabbalah. Although the Kabbalah is indeed a science, before the 20th century there was never an actual textbook. In order to fill in the gaps, Rav Yehuda Ashlag, the great Kabbalist who lived in Jerusalem from 1922 until his death in 1954, wrote a commentary on *The Zohar* and the texts of the Ari. He evolved while writing the commentaries, and published his primary work, *Talmud Eser Sefirot (The Study of the Ten Sefirot)*, considered the predominant study book of our time.

It is only in our days that the great Kabbalist, Rav Yehuda Ashlag, established the comprehensive and concise method suitable for all souls that descend to this world. Rav Yehuda Ashlag was born in Warsaw in 1885 and came to Jerusalem in 1922. He was appointed the rabbi of one of the neighborhoods in Jerusalem, and began to write *The Study of the Ten Sefirot*. He gave his composition this name because the spiritual world and this world, the souls in the Upper Worlds and indeed the entire universe, are all comprised of ten *Sefirot*.

This textbook of six volumes contains more than two thousand pages. It includes everything that Kabbalists have written since the dawn of time, from the writings of Adam (the First Man), Abraham the Patriarch, Moses, Rabbi Shimon Bar-Yochai to those of the holy Ari. This book displays Kabbalah in a concise manner, fit for study. Thus, we have with us today everything needed to learn how creation was made, how it comes down to us and how we can influence it from below all the way to the highest world, to have the future we desire. This is why today Kabbalists study only the books of Rav Yehuda Ashlag.

When we learn from *The Study of the Ten Sefirot* under the right conditions, meaning in the right way and under the right guidance, the Upper World opens. There is a special approach to the material in the book, and a special key that explains how to read the text, to make it open correctly. When we study in this way, we begin to feel the universe, to see and feel in every sense what exists beyond the range of our senses, because our senses are corporeal and limited, and can perceive nothing beyond their scope.

Kabbalist Rav Yehuda Ashlag writes in the introduction to *The Study of the Ten Sefirot* that, thanks to the permission he received from Above to write the book, anyone can attain the highest point of soul evolution in our world, and anyone can attain equivalence of form with the Upper Force, i.e. the Creator. We can attain the highest spiritual levels while living in this world, because the body no longer stands as a barrier between us and our souls. It doesn't matter if our soul is clothed in a body or not, because we can freely move from world to world, existing in all the worlds simultaneously, in a state of eternity and perfection. Then, we become timeless, motionless, and spaceless.

Baal HaSulam writes that by using his method, all these situations are attainable; he writes that his method is suitable for everyone without exception. Besides *The Study of the Ten Sefirot*, he also wrote a commentary on *The Zohar* and on the writings of the Ari. Baal HaSulam writes about himself, that he is a reincarnation of a soul that starts with the First Man, continues through Abraham the Patriarch, Moses, Rabbi Shimon Bar-Yochai, the Ari and finally to himself. Because of this, he could take the compositions of these Kabbalists, process them, and present them to us in way that suits our generation.

Although Baal HaSulam lived in our generation, what happened to his writings is much the same as what happened with *The Zohar* and the writings of the Ari: some of his writings were concealed and are only now being published.

And so the knowledge has been passed from one Kabbalist to the next. Through countless generations this great wisdom has flowed from giver to receiver, from mouth to mouth, and from teacher to student. This great legacy of teaching from Rav to disciple is presently expressed through two organizations, Bnei Baruch, carrying the name of Baruch Ashlag, and the Ashlag Research Institute (ARI). I am immensely honored to belong to both groups.

Why is Kabbalah learned in such a manner, passed down from teacher to student? The answer is simple: there is no other way. Kabbalah is a method, and that method is instruction in a process, not instruction in a philosophy or a religion. It is not a matter of discovery, but rather a matter of learning that process. For this reason, no one can discover the spiritual world alone.

Throughout the pages of this book, you will read words that I cannot claim, for the teachings within this book were handed down to me just as assuredly as they were presented to my teacher by his predecessors. This book is made up of the information from many articles, classes, private discussions, and books by my teacher Michael Laitman, or from those who have instructed him. True authorship of such information can never really be claimed, and even the style in which the material is presented has been strongly influenced by the style of that source of information.

This information is available to anyone and everyone who has the desire to open a book, to turn a page, and to listen to a lesson. Certainly one may pay a small price for the paper it is written on, as well as the cover that binds the pages of Kabbalistic texts, but the wisdom contained within those texts is priceless.

Why was this book written? Thomas Jefferson was once asked for why the Declaration of Independence was written. His reply—"To place before mankind the common sense of the subject in such terms as to command their ascent"—describes my exact purpose for this humble work.

The reader should not consider the book a textbook in learning Kabbalah, but rather an accurate introduction to the Wisdom. For readers wishing to further their studies in Kabbalah, Bnei Baruch provides a massive amount of information at the largest internet site in the world, www.kabbalah.info.

Bnei Baruch and the Ashlag Research Institute are non-profit organizations with a singular goal: to spread the Wisdom of Kabbalah throughout the world to all of humanity. Classes are provided to all levels of students via the internet and are absolutely free. Texts are currently provided in twenty-two languages.

CHAPTER 1.
WHY DID I PICK UP THIS BOOK?

Throughout the history of humankind, we as creatures have sought to find a way to live out this incredibly short existence all of us experience as "our lives" in a peaceful and tranquil manner. Yet for some reason the process seems to work backwards. Peace and tranquility seem to be present only in the first few years of our lives, followed by a long string of increasingly intense situations that lead us through a maze of chaos we call "adulthood."

As children, we begin with the tiniest cares, only for food, sleep and human warmth. Yet from the very first element of responsibility forced upon us, our lives begin a slow, yet persistent process of increasing stress and suffering, albeit usually interspersed with short pauses of joy and happiness.

Adolescence brings a myriad of internal and external changes, and along with them, a rollercoaster ride of emotional ups and downs. These highs and lows are felt so strongly that the average teenager can change from feeling like "my world is ending" to "what a wonderful life it is" several times a day, and usually does.

As young adults, we trade in one set of problems for an entirely different set. We meet that "significant other" with whom we will probably spend the majority of our lives. That union usually leads to additional expressions of love, not only increasing our joy, but our headaches, worries, and monthly expenditures as well.

As the years roll by, each seeming to move a little bit faster, we find that many of our original life endeavors have been traded for some element of security in order to provide for that now full household of loved ones. A stable career has become a necessity to provide for our family's needs and wants. Proper schooling is an absolute must in this age of high technology, and entertainment has become an American staple for escaping the stress associated with our relentless battles to nurture, provide, and enjoy.

One morning we awaken, look in the mirror, and find someone whose thick dark hair, once taken for granted, now boasts an additional shade we sometimes affectionately call "ultra blonde." That hard, lean body has miraculously grown a bit softer around the middle, and when we arise some parts just do not wake up as fast as others do. We find we have been struck with a condition that we have earned through years of strife: middle age. Again, responsibilities change, some falling away, some added on.

And as we see those years evaporate into the new environments of grandchildren and retirement, those events that once caused the hair to thin trade themselves for problems such as health, security, and even loneliness. We find our patience has grown longer and longer, and our goals are now slimmed down to realistic endeavors that do not require decades to complete.

But this incredible process called "life as we know it" can sometimes include an additional irritation. This particular annoyance can arise at any time in our lives, and with no apparent solution to its yearning. It is usually so subtle that at first we do not even recognize what the problem is. What is this troubling question with no apparent answer? It is a singular question, a wonderment that is both cruel, yet fair at the same time. That question is, "What is the meaning of my life?"

This question comes to us in a variety of forms.

"What am I doing on the planet?"

"Why is my life the way it is?"

"What am I supposed to be doing here? Is this it?"

Usually, we find this question intervening into our thoughts whenever we are going through a particularly demanding crisis. The intensity of this question is almost always directly related to the suffering we are experiencing at any given moment. The more we suffer, the louder it screams. For some of us on the planet, the question becomes so distinct and demanding that we begin to seek an answer.

At first, the search only brings additional questions like:

"What am I searching for?"
"Where do I start?"
"Can there really be more than just.......this?"

Our search leads us through myriad avenues, a multitude of solutions ranging from different physical exercises to strange cults, all promising in one way or another to satisfy our growing desire for what is usually deemed "the truth."

Those of us who suffer from this insatiable quest find ourselves attending this meeting or that lecture, reading a book or watching some video, always seeking a certain something we simply cannot put our finger on. We know we want, we just do not know exactly what it is that we want. There is a lack, an unfulfilled......something. The more we search, the more we attempt promised solutions for nullifying this "lack," the more frustrated we become when the promised solution turns out to steal our time or—worse—lighten our wallets.

This book was written for all of you who know exactly what I am talking about, for those who have experienced this "lack." If you should find yourself in the above description commonly referred to as "seekers," then most assuredly that is the reason you have opened this book.

Seekers can be found in every social stratum. You may find them in the most horrendous of circumstances, poverty stricken, having suffered from calamities too numerous to count, or you may find them at the other end of the spectrum. How often have we heard stories of people who seemingly have everything—money, respect, possessions, friends, family—yet they have just checked themselves into a rehabilitation facility, or worse.

Often those who literally "have it all" find that in the end, they do not. In fact, they would trade all they have for something they simply cannot put their finger on. They know something is missing, but literally have no clue as to what it is. Therefore, they turn to drugs, relationships, and an array of superficial pleasures to satiate this constantly growing "lack."

Finally, there are many of us who have not suffered a great tragedy. Certainly, most of us have had our share of suffering, but as a rule we are reasonably comfortable. We work at our daily jobs, feed and support our families, and lead "normal" lives. Yet that lack seems to tingle within, teasing and taunting us. It drives us to search, and search we do.

No matter what your situation, this book offers to help provide some of those answers you are seeking. Its aim is twofold: first, to explain the source of the lack you feel within. Second, to help you discover the solution to this feeling of lack. This world offers no fulfillment or solution to your question, and no answer to satiate your thirst, as what you lack is not available here. By "here" I am referring to the world in which you live. Your sense of lack reveals not only a lack, but a need for discovery.

This brings about the question, "What in the world needs to be discovered?" Have we not discovered just about everything there is to discover on this planet? Have we not begun to explore the heavens? Are medical miracles not being found to a huge variety of ailments every single day? Are our computers not so lightening fast already that we can communicate instantly around the world, thanks to this incredible new toy called "the internet?"

What is left to discover?

The object of discovery is a realm we do not yet occupy. It is the realm of sources, desires, feelings and thoughts. It is the realm of the Creator, and it is simply called "spirituality."

CHAPTER 2.
SPIRITUALITY

Spirituality. The very word causes a cavalcade of descriptions, ranging from what we find at the bottom of a bottle of tequila, to religion, to cults, to ghosts and goblins. Yet what is this thing we call "spirituality?" Is it a place such as heaven? Is it a religion such as Christianity, Judaism or Islam? Is it a condition? Is it a state of mind? Or is it a combination of all of the above?

If we consider the lack from which we suffer, we can narrow it down a bit. Whatever spirituality is, it is definitely not here, not in this world where we live, eat, sleep, breath, and fulfill a generous amount of our desires. The topic has been discussed, refuted, pontificated upon, buried, and resurrected more times than can be counted. Yet for whatever reason, a singular definition of "spirituality" still eludes us.

Having been examined from a variety of directions, most everyone agrees on one fact: spirituality is where the "soul" resides. In other words, it is the soul's environment. That is all well and good, but it also defines nothing until we know what a soul is. It is like saying to someone from a different planet that "this item is a dog house" yet they have no idea what a dog is.

In general, there are four common attitudes regarding the soul, as well as our existence here in the physical and the spiritual. Those four attitudes are religious, secular, scientific, and philosophical. The following description is taken from Attaining the Worlds Beyond and offers a brief explanation of each:

RELIGIOUS DEFINITION OF SPIRITUALITY

Clothed within each and every one of our physical bodies is an eternal entity called a "soul." The soul is eternal, and as an object has virtually nothing to do with the world in which we physically live, unless it inhabits a body. It has a completely independent existence from

22

the physical body and exists before, during and after the physical body's existence.

The soul is not a "body" as we know it, having no organs or physical attributes, and can therefore be considered "whole" or undivided. It is much like dividing a pitcher of water into three glasses; the water in each of the glasses still contains every element of the original substance, missing nothing. The soul does contain certain qualities that it expresses when clothed within a physical body. Furthermore, the physical body takes on the spiritual qualities of the soul while the soul inhabits it.

The body itself is simply a physical and biological substance with no characteristics of its own until the soul inhabits it. The inhabiting by a soul within a body is called physical "birth" and the leaving of a soul from a physical body is called "death." Without the soul, the body could not move or interact in any way because the soul is responsible for the body's life and motion.

SECULAR

This approach is also known as the "dualistic" approach to explain the soul's existence, as well as to explain our physical existence. Most college students who have taken biology classes are very familiar with an experiment that has been repeated many times. Under the right conditions, gaseous and solid chemicals are mixed within a vacuum chamber, an electrical spark is induced and presto, instant life appears. The discovery of such science has led to an expansion of the initial religious idea. It goes something like this:

Certainly souls do inhabit bodies, but they do not necessarily have to in order for the physical body to exist. The biological body can exist as a totally independent unit, able to perform all functions of life. It exhibits qualities of its own, albeit none that are spiritual. But here is the catch. In order to actually have any spiritual qualities, the soul must inhabit the body, just like in the original religious concept. And since the soul is a spiritual entity, the body is the recipient of only good qualities when inhabited by the soul. Otherwise, it is simply like any other animal, until that point when it is inhabited by the soul. But the soul is the actual controlling force because it is what causes the body to be born and maintains it as well.

SCIENTIFIC

This approach is also known as the "non-believer" attitude. Basically this idea denies any existence of a soul or spirituality altogether. In fact, the only thing that exists is what is here, what can be seen or detected physically. Every event the body performs is a function of calculations of the brain with regard to pain and pleasure. Data is received through our senses and analyzed by the brain, which then determines whether what is being sensed causes pain or pleasure.

The brain also has the ability to store information regarding what it has experienced as pain or pleasure. It attempts to recreate the situations of pleasure over and over again. The reverse is also true with regard to pain. So in this concept, almost everything operates by example and memory. Of course, the brain can guess from what it perceives as pleasure that something similar will produce pleasure as well.

So in this view, what separates us from animals? The difference between us and, say, the devoted pet that lies at your feet is simply the advanced development of the human brain. The human brain analyzes and acts on hundreds of thousands of times more data than that of your animal companion. This massive amount of analysis is how we "reason" and is responsible for our superiority over every other creature.

This reason stems from both the amount of data we can process, and the speed at which we process it. Hence, animals are categorized by the volume and speed they analyze and process. Of course, this approach is far and away the most scientific. It relies totally on what we have in front of us, what we can see or detect with scientific experiments. The basis for every action or non-action we make is the processing of data that comes to us through our environment.

The downside to this approach is that this removes any romantic idea of humankind and relegates us to being mere slaves of our environment, constantly calculating pleasure versus pain. Any concept of free will goes right out the window as all our actions are merely a combination of our initial genetic makeup and our environment. From this great conundrum, lacking appeal to most scientists, came the final attempt to create the more palatable approach we refer to as "philosophical."

PHILOSOPHICAL

The "philosophical" or "modern" concept takes the best of all three concepts and attempts to provide an explanation for our physical and spiritual existence. Yes, the soul does exist. Yes, the soul is the real "us." Yes, the soul is an eternal and spiritual being. Yes, our genetic makeup and environment strongly affect how we are here. Of course, once again, we have raised many more questions than we have answered, even if we combine all three of these definitions.

At the end of the day, the three concepts that accept the existence of the soul fail to explain how it is related to the body in this world. We are most comfortable with what we can see, hear, smell, touch, and feel. Yet the scientific version of spirituality leaves this incredibly strong sense of lack completely unanswered. What most of us end up doing is fantasizing about the spiritual, simply assuming it exists. Those who believe there is nothing but what we have here are few and far between, for who wants to believe their existence ends at physical death?

Here we find ourselves struggling with an age-old dichotomy. We want to believe in spirituality and the soul, but we have absolutely nothing concrete to base it on. If we apply our normal reasoning to the problem, our logical conclusion is too painful for most of us to stomach. To break down the problem to the basics, we cannot logically say we "accept" the existence of something unless we actually experience it. Our only solution would be to somehow experience the perception of something spiritual, yet we have no concrete real way of perceiving what we define as the "spiritual"...or do we?

Nearly everyone has an opinion about what spirituality is, but almost no one has any connection with the spiritual world or any idea how it works. People have argued that the spiritual can be understood through arts such as music, or through science, religion, even psychology. But spirituality can really only be understood when experienced. This means that a person must somehow be able to enter the "place of the spiritual," research it, and determine what its properties are. In other words, they must undertake a process of discovery. The tool for this process is called "Kabbalah."

Kabbalah is a clear, concise system that helps us to discover what that mysterious lack is, and then provides a proven method to fill it. One cannot attain the spiritual through psychological or other earthly means. Methods that involve meditation or special music certainly do produce psychological phenomena that make us feel wonderful, but that is not the spirituality to which I am referring.

The spiritual world I refer to can only be revealed through a wisdom that serves as a branch, a lifeline, a connection between "here" and "there." Our world, as well as that of the spiritual, operates through forces. The study of the method of Kabbalah is a complex system comprised of one's own work, by which one draws upon oneself a very special and unique force.

That special force Kabbalah refers to as "Light" awakens the spiritual desire in us, a desire to fill the lack that originally brought us to search for answers. That lack is our wish to continue living in this world, but primarily from a physical perspective in the animate body. What changes is everything that has to do with our minds and our desires; they should operate on an altogether different frequency, as if one were breaking through an invisible barrier to another world.

This kind of spiritual discovery that we generally coin "attainment" cannot be seen, presented, or made apparent to anyone. People who have not experienced it cannot feel or comprehend the explanations for it. Attainment is a unique, completely intimate feeling, a sensation that is attained through the study of this wondrous wisdom.

Simply put, Kabbalah is a method that allows a person to experience and research the spiritual. In doing so, one discovers and reaches many different spiritual degrees and states. The process that enables us to have these incredible insights stems from a spiritual concept called "equivalence of form," which will be described in detail in this book.

To begin with, let's start with a brief overview of exactly what is contained within the spiritual. There are basically two elements and one process. These two elements are the Creator and the creature. The process is a method similar to a machine that starts with these two elements, separated as far from each other as east is from west. Through a successive series of spiritual steps, the creature slowly moves closer to its Creator. By doing so, more and more of the Creator is gradually revealed.

THE CREATOR

The Wisdom of Kabbalah, our tool for research, utilizes its own specific language in order to describe certain aspects of the spiritual. For instance, terms such as God, Creator, and Emanator are actually labels of specific forces and degrees. The different names of God used within the Wisdom simply describe our perception of a single Force from a different perspective than previously experienced. In other words, the difference between one spiritual degree and another is not that the Creator has changed; it is just that a bit more of Him has been revealed because *we* have changed.

Many who first begin their studies are under the misconception that Kabbalah refers to more than one Force, but it does not. They ask, "Does this infer that there is not one singular Force, one supreme Force in the entire universe?" To the contrary, it is our changing perspective that causes this illusion that there is more than one Force and different Lights – these are different perceptions of the Creator.

We experience one degree at a time, so whatever we experience as the next higher degree we always perceive as the Creator. In fact, as we discover a degree, it will appear so perfect, so right, that we find it virtually impossible to think there is anything else but this degree. Our experience is, "This is it, I have found it all." Yet, as time passes, another layer will be added, provided that we keep working towards it.

One can also look at this process from another point of view. The Creator can also be thought of as the Collection of the Forces we discover, the Sum of the parts. This Collective Force actually monitors the whole system of creation. From this perspective, the Creator is One and is completely unique. This Force, the Creator, has but one singular mission, to delight His creatures in any possible way they can be delighted. This is considered the one primary law of the spiritual worlds.

Every other law is a branch of that law, which cascades downward and is responsible for everything that happens. How should we regard this law? The simplest answer is that every single thing that happens to you every second of the day has but one sole purpose: to bring you to the point of utter bliss, and to be completely filled with the Light of the Creator.

Kabbalah breaks down the structure of the spiritual into pieces, then pieces of pieces. One can also visualize the overall structure as a five-layered onion. In the center is the heart, the Creator. We, the souls, are on the very outside of that onion. We are concealed from the Creator by these five general layers, which Kabbalah calls "worlds."

One can think of these layers as coverings, or veils, that hide what's inside. The first layer of the onion, the first world, is called *Adam Kadmon*. The successive worlds, additional layers between the Creator and us, Kabbalah gives the names *Atzilut, Beria, Yetzira,* and *Assiya,* the outermost layer.

From the innermost point, the heart of the onion, the Creator pulls us toward Him. If we place a cannonball on our bed, then another smaller ball at the edge of the bed, we will observe that the smaller ball plunges downward toward the cannonball. Of course, we all know we have just witnessed the effect of gravity. The Creator acts very much like this force, constantly pulling His creatures closer to Him.

When we, as His creatures, feel that tug, the pull inward, we normally sense it as pain. That pain is the result of our resistance. But when we begin to cooperate with that Force and work with it in order to come closer to the Creator, we will no longer feel any pain. Instead, the Force will become a source of pleasure. It will feel good. Of course, the antithesis is correct as well. The more we resist, the more pain we feel. This is the source of our troubles and the troubles society experiences as a whole.

So we can look at Kabbalah in a different way. Its wondrous wisdom provides a manner in which to view ourselves so that no matter what the situation or circumstance, we are always in agreement with that Force. In so doing, we are always headed in the right direction, towards the Creator. Hence, although Kabbalah does provide answers to our desires in our world, it has an even more important purpose: to give us an impression of a new reality that opens before us, a new life that will fulfill us.

To equalize with the Creator means to be equal to Him in every manifestation. It does not refer to the Upper Force itself, but to how He relates to things, how He appears before us, within us, as a Supreme Power, as Essence, in the way that He wants us to feel Him. Another word of caution is in order here. The above does not mean we become God or that we are God. It simply means that when we enter the spiritual, we have been able to equalize with the *attribute* of the Creator (i.e. bestowal), not His essence. This confusion has led to major misunderstandings where people think, "We are God."

The Creator created us from His wish to give, to bestow. He created our will to receive exactly in the amount that He wanted to give. That is why we must attain everything that He wants to give us – eternity, strength, perfection, total control. So our target is to obtain those same characteristics.

The primary law of creation is the singularity of the Creator—the one and only Power that controls everything. There is none else beside Him And that Power is one of bestowal.

The second law of creation is that the Creator is totally benevolent.

We cannot settle the contradiction between these two laws as they appear in our conception of reality. If we explore the world around us, it surely doesn't seem as if the Creator is being benevolent. But people who achieve that equivalence of form will tell you that this is no theory, but pure fact. How do they know this? They discover this fact within that sensation of the Creator. People who enter the spiritual and are working on achieving that equivalence of form are called "Kabbalists."

The work they perform is called "correction." This correction is not like the correction of a child who has misbehaved, but more like the correction made when we fine tune the dial on a radio, thereby receiving the station more clearly. There will be much more about that later.

THE CREATURE

As creatures, we are at the very center of the Creator's creation. We were created for only one purpose: to first establish contact with Him, then to begin a relationship with Him. Of course, our ultimate goal is to realize, meaning to make real, His sole purpose, to delight His creation. We accomplish this task through a process called "correction," meaning to achieve equivalence of form.

The correction of a person makes it possible to be filled with the Light of the Creator, meaning to feel the Creator. This sensation is exactly where we experience the spiritual worlds. To accomplish our task, we must be completely filled with the Creator. We start from a state that Kabbalah calls "this world," where The Creator is totally concealed from us.

The spiritual worlds are measures of concealment of the Creator from His creatures. In order to hammer home this point, let me repeat that the spiritual worlds are not worlds as we think of them in corporality. They are simply tools of measurement, their labels akin to signs of different levels of concealment of the Creator.

Our initial perception, that first contact, is considered the ascent of the soul to the first spiritual degree. What happens next? The soul continues the process of correction, making it resemble the Creator more and more. Of course, with each degree attained, we feel the Creator that much more strongly. Then, at some point, we reach a final step of our personal correction. Kabbalah calls that *Gmar Tikkun*, or the "end of correction" of the soul.

THE CORRECTION

The desire to enjoy that which was created by the Creator is called a "creature," or the "substance" of creation. However, this desire cannot be fulfilled in its primary form because as soon as one is filled with pleasure, the joy vanishes. Anyone who has ever dived into a massive portion of their favorite dessert has experienced this very phenomenon. The more of the delicious treat we eat, the less we enjoy it. In fact, if we eat enough, we will end up sick of it.

So there is a problem. The desires we experience are incomplete. The intent of the Creator from the start was to make the desire complete. However, this only happens when our intent resembles the Creator's attribute of bestowal by our free choice. Because this attribute is not limited in its use by emotions, we can attain perfection and eternity. One can get tired of the dessert, but if one feels pleasure by giving it away, then the pleasure simply continues to grow, never negating the desire.

Correction means that each person is obliged to transform the will for self-enjoyment into the will to please the Creator. By performing this single task, the result is that our desire to enjoy precisely equals the Creator's desire to give us pleasure. The primary point here is that the

Creator is bringing His creation to a point where it can actually use its only attribute, the will to receive, in a correct manner.

Thus, the correction pertains only to the correction of the aim over the desires that appear within a person. In other words, for every single desire that appears in a person, he or she must eventually use it to benefit others.

It is important to note that these corrections cannot be performed by the creature, but rather by the Creator. In other words, they are performed by a higher spiritual degree then our current one. We never have the strength to perform self-corrections. We must simply cultivate a desire to be corrected, which is a prayer for correction, to a certain degree of intensity. The Creator will take care of the rest. The next upper degree will perform it. Those who are undergoing or have undergone this process of correction are called "Kabbalists."

For true correction, we must choose a place that we feel in our hearts is exactly the right place for us. This need not be because of the presence of a great teacher, one who is highly regarded by others, and not because that teacher is eloquent and knowledgeable. One must choose a place where things are spoken that one wishes to know in one's heart.

So what should we do when we begin to realize our purpose and the need to fulfill it? How do we begin this process of revealing the Creator? We should search in our hearts and be honest with ourselves, agreeing to nothing unless we think it right. This includes even the smallest thing, because the soul must find the place where it will be corrected.

The first question most people who discover this lack ask is, "What is the sensation of the Creator like?" The sensation of the Creator cannot be put into words accurately. Why? We simply have no words to describe it, though it is a very tangible sensation indeed, as it is written: "Taste and see that the Lord is good."

CHAPTER 3.
DESIRE - THE FUEL THAT DRIVES US

Do we eat because we are hungry or because we want *not* to be hungry? Do we scratch our noses because they itch, or because we want them to stop itching? When we were teenagers, did we clean our rooms instead of doing something fun because we wanted to clean our rooms, or because we wanted not to have a parent who was mad at us? I could go on and on with these rhetorical questions, but I think most readers will see where this is heading.

Every single act we perform in life is born out of a desire. From the smallest, most insignificant, conscious act to acts that require a vast amount of energy, they are all performed for one single reason: a desire entered us and affected us enough for us to take an action to fulfill it. Kabbalah calls the Force that propels us to fulfill these desires "the will to receive."

We are completely controlled by desire; without one, we remain perfectly still, not moving as much as an inch. But what is the goal? What are we trying to achieve by consciously and subconsciously following our desires? The answer is pleasure. We pursue them in order to receive pleasure in one form or another.

Sometimes that pleasure may be the feeling of doing something because we believe it is the right thing to do. Other times it may be at the expense of another's happiness. But no matter what the desire, it is the same will to receive that is the underlying force, literally leading us around by the nose to act in a manner that fulfills the desire.

This will to receive is so complex and cunning that at best we barely even notice we are slaves to it. Of course, nobody in their right mind wishes to admit they are a slave to anything or anybody. But if a person takes time to seriously reflect why he or she performs any given action, even actions of the highest morality, there is only one conclusion that explains all acts. We act only in order to receive pleasure for ourselves.......period.

This is an exceptionally hard axiom to grasp. As a teacher of Kabbalah, I find most beginning students struggle with such a concept. I instantly receive a litany of examples from students trying to show that the above statement is dead wrong. Some of these examples include the millions of people who give to charities every day, a man throwing himself on a hand grenade during a war to save kids, Mother Theresa building orphanages for children, the list is virtually endless. Yet when I ask them why they think these people did what they did, the final answer is not "to save kids' lives." It's because the person who did the deed felt it was the right thing to do.

In other words, in these people's judgment, the correct act was determined to be exactly what they did. In fact, each person in each example was doing something that may even have had a negative impact or caused great sacrifice for themselves, but they would not have been happy with any other action. For instance, in the hand grenade example, the soldier had placed the value of the children's lives above his own, therefore making it impossible *not* to perform the act he did.

The will to receive pleasure is so powerful that it can even override instant gratification, such as safety or money, for a greater pleasure to be received in the future. At the end of the day, if we have any stake in an outcome, if we calculated ways to achieve this result, our will to receive made that decision.

So what really happens with the will to receive and why does it cause such actions when a desire presents itself? The answer is simple—a judgment is made. A calculation occurs regarding the pleasure an act may bring versus alternative actions and the pleasure they may bring. This calculation happens at lightning speed and does not usually require conscious thought. What ingenious tool has such a capability to perform these calculations and do it literally millions of times a day? The answer lies right between our ears: that marvel of a biological computer we refer to as the brain. We will speak more about this miraculous calculating machine in a moment.

The will to receive is so perfectly developed within us that it boggles the mind to consider how many acts it controls every single second. Every function of your body operates through this environment. All systems act in a coordinated manner to insure the utmost efficiency for a person's bare survival on an unconscious level; all the while calculations that require conscious cognitive processing occur simultaneously.

Every second, and every move we make, whether swinging in our office chairs to help ease stress or bringing our wives flowers after work, is a desire to receive that is designed, analyzed, and calculated before any action ever takes place. Most of this process goes completely unnoticed without any cognitive effort. Just sit back and think for a moment how many individual movements it takes to get up and get a glass of water when we are thirsty.

Of course, there is calculation there as well. Enter the brain. Our biological systems detect a desire for water, so we feel thirsty. Now we may or may not go and get the glass of water. That depends on the calculations of the brain. For instance, if we are sitting in front of the television watching our favorite show or a particularly exciting ball game, we might forego that desire, at least until the next advertisement.

What happened? The brain made a calculation, weighing the pleasure we would receive by getting out of the chair now and going to get the water versus the pleasure we receive from what we are watching. If the subject here is a man, and his wife is watching her favorite soap opera, he will not hesitate to get up and get the water. But if it is the World Series and his favorite team is playing, the water can wait.

The calculation with regard to when or whether to perform an action at all is a calculation of work. That is the fundamental formula within the brain: possible pleasure received versus work required to receive the pleasure. If we are sick as a dog lying in bed at night sleeping and the phone rings, we probably will not get out of bed to answer it. But if the house is on fire and we smell smoke, we can literally be on our death beds, but we will get out of that house somehow. The brain prioritizes. It matches, compares, estimates and makes the decision based upon the results of the analysis. Once the decision has been made, only then is there an action.

In the case of desires like the thirst for water, it is easy to see how the will to receive works. The confusion comes when we begin to consider acts where a person is seemingly giving to others, like people who support charities, or Boy Scouts who help old ladies cross the street. The answer is that there are actually two types of receiving for oneself.

The first is the simplest: the will to receive in order to receive. The second is the will to give in order to receive. As previously mentioned, the will to receive is exceptionally cunning. Not only can it work out ways to receive by simply getting for itself, it can even work out ways to receive by giving to others.

On the surface, this makes absolutely no sense. What possible pleasure could one receive by giving? Of course, anyone who has ever been to a birthday party, brought a gift to a friend, and laid it upon the table with the rest of the gifts is well aware how they simply cannot wait for their friend to open the particular gift they had brought. In fact, it is of uttermost importance that the gift they brought is enjoyed by the birthday honoree. If not, there is a deep sense of sorrow, a disappointment that is very hard to explain. In point of fact, we receive a certain type of pleasure for an act of giving as well.

Some people have discovered just how pleasurable this type of receiving can be and literally give millions of dollars to charities all over the world. It is not that they necessarily like dispensing their hard-earned money; it is simply that they receive a pleasure that is greater by doing so than by keeping it and spending it on themselves. In fact, some people are so addicted to this type of pleasure that, if you were to somehow stop them from continuing to do so, they would no longer consider life worth living.

It is important to note here that Kabbalah does not say that people who receive in order to receive or give in order to receive are evil in any way. In fact, it is quite the opposite and there is a special reason for it. You see, those desires causing such actions come directly from the

Creator. Every day people simply follow the program under which they were created. Like a sophisticated computer program that says "if yes, do this, if no, do that," they merrily march on day in and day out receiving desires, calculating, and fulfilling—or not—depending on the results of the calculation.

People receive their desires from two distinct places. First, there are the animal desires, which are the same as those of any other biological animal. These desires for food, rest, shelter, and procreation are received genetically and are apparent no matter whether one lives within society or not. What do we really need? We need a slab of meat to chew on, a cave to stay out of the elements and to rest, a partner to fulfill physical desires and desires for procreation, just like any other animal.

Then society takes over. There are desires such as money, honor, knowledge, and power that we depend upon society to provide. What do these offer us? Money determines whether or not we eat that slab of meat or we enjoy a wonderful filet mignon at Ruth's Chris. It determines whether we stay in that cave or live in a 20-room mansion, or something in between. Sometimes, it even determines the partner we choose.

Everybody wants to feel good about themselves, and if left totally alone, this does not take much effort. Yet this is where the society really begins to come into play. How? Our opinion regarding our self-worth is drastically influenced by how we are regarded by the society we live in. It is no wonder that the homeless, the unemployed, and those with drug problems have little or no self-esteem. All one has to do is observe how society views such people.

Then there is our immediate environment. We have all experienced the "keeping up with the Jones'" syndrome. If our immediate environment dictates that it's important to have a certain type of car, you will see garages full of them. If it is a certain hairstyle, every woman will be wearing it. If hunting is what determines one's manliness in the area, hunting will be a popular sport. In other words, our society provides us with what it deems important in these areas.

Today, a college education is a virtual necessity. In fact, its value more closely compares with the value of a high school education years ago when a college diploma was considered a "head start." In today's world of high tech, the post-graduate degree is the head start.

But if one moves to a poverty-stricken country and is left there with no possessions, simple survival issues will be deemed of greatest importance. Eating, drinking, and shelter might be regarded as honorable, while education will mean virtually nothing, except to perhaps escape this challenging environment.

Of course, we do have some freedom of choice. Our current fashions will offer a variety of colors and shapes, the latest type of car will come in different models by different companies, and we have a wide array of choices for that college degree. But even in these, our choices are based on desire, what we perceive will give us the most pleasure. If something within me makes me prefer green, chances are my car is going to be green. Why? Because I feel better with a green car.

To summarize, every action we make is predetermined by the desires within each and every one of us. We receive those desires from two different sources: our genetics and our environment. We are pressured one way or the other to fulfill what we calculate will bring us the most pleasure based upon those desires we receive. To go against these pressures is virtually impossible.

Desires from society enter into us through our five senses. When we smell apple pie, a desire that was previously not there appears. Is there anyone who has ever eaten just one potato chip, and not reached for another? The sense of taste immediately kicks in and out of the blue, we feel our life will be incomplete without that next chip.

But there is one more desire; the desire brought up in the first chapter of this book. What is that desire and where is it from? Why does it at first tease us, then annoy us, and finally drive us to seek answers? What is the fundamental basis for this desire and how can we fulfill it? Who really are we? The answer lies in a single discovery of that spiritual entity called "the soul!"

CHAPTER 4.
A POINT IN THE HEART - THE SOUL

So what is the great mystery of the soul, and exactly what is it?

The soul is a desire created by the Creator to enjoy Him (the Light). It is actually in perfect adhesion with the Creator, just as it was when it was first created. But the soul needs to accomplish this situation in its own right, to actually obtain an equivalence of form independently, and in so doing become like its Creator. In order to accomplish this task, the Creator completely separates the soul from Himself. This happens by giving the soul the exact opposite attribute that He possesses - the will to receive again.

Through this disparity of form, the soul stops sensing the Creator and is clothed in a corporeal body with the will to receive pleasure purely for its own sake. So if the soul does not sense the Creator, what does it sense? It senses "our world," the very place that we consider our entire existence. In order to achieve that original state again, when it was complete and sensed the Creator, the soul must take on the task of attaining those attributes of the Creator. It does this through a process that is akin to giving birth to them, creating them itself.

The soul, as it exists in "our world," is no more than a point. From this single point we can only perceive our own will, which is to delight the corporeal bodies within which we reside. Yet from this point, remote as it can possibly be from the Creator, we are at the perfect place to start our journey back toward the Creator. It is important here not to confuse the soul with the will to receive for ourselves, our current condition. Remember that the soul is a singular desire to enjoy the Creator. In a way, the soul is like a part of the Creator. It's just that the Creator is the whole, and the soul is a part.

Everyone has a soul existing within them. When we first become aware of it, the soul is felt as a point in the heart, at the center of all desires, in our ego. But at what level is this soul? That is something we must all discover. We see millions of people all over the world with absolutely no recognizable desire except to fulfill their own wants. Within these people exists the soul as well, yet in an embryonic state. Kabbalah calls this soul, "a point in the heart."

In this instance, the heart is the desire to take pleasure in everything around us. And that point is the one single desire out of all other desires a person possesses that is *not* a desire for worldly pleasures. It is the desire to reveal its Creator.

Humans develop desires for physical pleasures, and then for wealth, power, control, and knowledge. After those desires for worldly pleasures, generally called the "heart," is the desire for spirituality. This desire is the end of the line, where nothing in this world can possibly fulfill that lack.

The desire for spirituality seems to appear within the animate desires, hence the name, "point in the heart." Of course, those desires have nothing to do with the heart in our bodies. If we implanted a new heart in someone, it would not change a single characteristic in that person— even if we implanted a new brain. The spiritual sphere has nothing to do with our biological bodies.

The point in the heart is not really considered the soul, but the "soul in potential." At this stage, it resembles a lack that simply cannot be filled. We know we want something, we know we are missing something, but for the life of us, we cannot figure out what we need. The point in the heart is like a drop of desire, a yearning for supreme attainment, for the Creator. If a person begins to develop it, it grows like the sperm that has fertilized a human egg and now has evolved into a fetus. When it becomes independent, it is called a "soul."

The process of the development and birth of the soul can be favorably compared to the same process that occurs in human beings. The soul is born out of a spiritual seed, which is developed by the Light that descends on a person when studying Kabbalah. The point in the heart then begins to inflate and expand under the influence of that Light, and finally evolves into ten complete attributes Kabbalah calls *Sefirot*; the complete structure of the soul is called a *Partzuf*, or a *Guf* (body) of a soul. The Upper Light (the sensation of the Creator by the creature) is drawn into those ten attributes, or *Sefirot*. This is how a person begins to feel the spiritual world, the Upper One, the Creator.

The soul is the desire to delight in the Creator. In other words, it is the desire to receive the Light that comes from Him. A desire to receive is called a Vessel, or *Kli*. The purpose of the Creator is to satisfy that desire for pleasure within the soul, provided the soul itself wants it. When that happens, it will feel pleasure. The Creator solved the problem of the soul wanting to feel pleasure by distancing the soul from Him. When the soul moves away from the Creator, it begins to want to draw near Him of its own accord. That gradually creates in it the desire for Him.

The created soul is called *Adam*. It is, in fact, the one and only creation, a desire to receive pleasure from the Creator. The original soul is divided into 600,000 parts. A hologram serves as a good example to show that each randomly taken part of the spiritual realm consists of all the other parts, only in miniature proportions according to the part's level.

Each part of the soul evolves gradually from that initial concealed point to a vast spiritual Vessel (620 times greater), over the course of 6,000 consecutive corrections, called "years" or "degrees." Again, it is important not to confuse the term "years" with our earthly term; it is a measurement of corrections, not time. We will talk more about these numbers later.

In the beginning of one's spiritual journey in this world, there is a change in a person's desires: the desire to delight in pleasures of this world turns into a desire to delight in the Creator. This is the greatest egoistic desire of all.

There is an initial level of egoism that conceals spirituality from us called "the barrier." Once beyond the barrier and inside the spiritual world, each part of the soul goes through a transformation from the intent for me to "for the Creator." This transformation Kabbalah calls a "correction." The extent of this correction is the extent of fulfillment with the Light of the Creator until the soul is finally and completely full. That sensation cannot be described in words; it is a sensation of eternity, wholeness, equivalence of form with the Creator. It is the purpose of creation.

Everyone is born into this world with the same five senses: seeing, hearing, feeling, tasting and smelling. Since we all have the same senses, we all see this corporeal world in the same way. But what are we really feeling through these senses? We are feeling our desire to enjoy, the desire for pleasure. This desire manifests in all five senses at once and is experienced on five different levels:

1. Animate pleasures from sex, family and food.
2. Pleasure from wealth and social status.
3. Pleasure from power (control) and fame.
4. Pleasure from knowledge.
5. Pleasure from the Creator.

Of course, we are all built a bit differently; we all aspire to different forms of pleasure. One person may wish to be a teacher, another wants to be a lawyer, and yet another might wish to drive a truck. These differences are all based upon the different combinations of those desires appearing within each of us. And according to the proportion of desires within our collective desire, each of us experiences different feelings. This is where the uniqueness of people comes from.

Now let's return to the *Sefirot* for a moment. *Sefirot* are attributes that are given to the creature, through which to feel the Creator. That is why the *Sefirot* express supremacy. They are attributes that the Creator wants His creatures to attain in order for them to feel Him. The entire universe is comprised of ten *Sefirot*, each comprised of ten inner *Sefirot*, and so on, indefinitely. For that reason, each particle in the universe will always be comprised of ten parts, or *Sefirot*. But the proportions between the parts are always unique to that particle.

Think for a moment about how we get to know someone. Obviously, at first we are only in contact with a person visually. But as we get to know them, their ways and inner attributes, we discover what is behind that outer body, what their inner attributes are. The external part of a person is only needed for the purpose of providing a sort of outer dressing for those inner attributes.

We can say that we truly know a person only after we know all his or her attributes and reactions in varying situations. Kabbalah calls the process of getting to know the Creator, "attaining the Creator." A person attains the Creator through the *Sefirot*, meaning through the Creator's outer appearances and His attributes. Through the *Sefirot* we will ultimately come to know reality, which is all a dressing for the Creator, just as our bodies are a dressing for our souls.

The Creator works inside us, in our souls. So if we learn to attain the Creator, we do it by discovering His actions in our soul. In other words, we attain the Creator by the action of the Light on our point in the heart, the desire to reveal the Creator. That point is not empty, although it is felt that way, but rather is filled with goodness. However, in order to feel it, we need to experience every emotion, and only then do we learn to feel the Light as it enters a specific point in the soul. This brings a very special feeling that can only be described as "completeness."

Completeness is a pleasure that is sensed only after there is a hunger for something and a shortage of it. I ate a cookie yesterday and remember how it tasted. I want one today and that desire is experienced as incompleteness. In other words, I remember the pleasure of eating that cookie and I now feel a lack. I can only fulfill that lack to the extent of the incompleteness I feel before I devour another cookie today.

Of course, tomorrow I will probably want another cookie. This is because nature has arranged lack and fulfillment, hunger and satisfaction, where they do not occur at the same time. This is the exact situation the Creator has placed our souls in to feel the lack, feel incomplete and thereby crave pleasure. As a result, we learn we most certainly can satisfy a lack or hunger, but we can never get our fill. No matter how many bags of cookies I buy, when the bag of cookies runs out, I will definitely be running to the store to pick up another bag.

Luckily, the Creator has a solution for this situation. He wants to delight us, which is why He sends us a very special fulfillment. Our souls try not to spoil that satisfaction by crossing the line and devouring the whole bag. It is only in this way that the soul arrives at completeness. The hunger and desire do not go away—on the contrary. As a result of this special fulfillment, the soul extends more fulfillment from a wholeness that does not fade, an eternal wholeness.

How does this special fulfillment work? I enjoy eating that cookie because prior to ripping open the bag, I feel a hunger, a lack, a sensation of shortage. In other words, I want a cookie. After I eat a few cookies, I no longer want any more because the lack has been fulfilled. But in the spiritual, the Creator gave our souls a great "trick" that prevents it from being satiated, despite the reception of pleasure. The more full our souls feel, the hungrier they grow. That is the perfection of the action of the Creator.

True pleasure, real pleasure, lasts as long as the desire lasts—it is insatiable. But on the spiritual level, when the desire to enjoy receives, it feels shame. You see, the soul does not just sense the pleasure, but also senses the attributes of the Giver. As it senses the Giver, it finds it not only wants the pleasure, but also wishes to relate to the Giver, to be like Him. The moment pleasure is felt from receiving, the pleasure begins to fade. The very act of the soul receiving for itself restricts the pleasure. That is why we cannot attain eternal delight by receiving, because receiving restricts the Light and even extinguishes it, virtually nullifying it.

Kabbalah calls the spiritual sensation of shame "hell." There is nothing worse than this sensation of shame because it's the same as being totally opposite from the Creator. The Creator purposely paired receiving with shame. He could have avoided it, but the phenomenon of shame was created specifically for us so we could learn to receive from Him, to delight without shame.

To our soul's dismay, the very act of receiving what it wants most causes the pleasure received to vanish into thin air. But the Creator has provided a wonderful solution. It turns out that the only way for the soul to receive pleasure is to enjoy not the pleasure itself, but rather our contact with the Giver of the pleasure. If the pleasure from contact with the Giver is what you get from Him, then your pleasure will not disappear and will not diminish your desire for pleasure. On the contrary! The more you receive, the more you give, and the more you enjoy. That process lasts indefinitely!!!

Think about the first time you met someone and fell head over heels in love with them. At first, it did not matter what you did or what they did—you simply received pleasure from being with them. Their very presence made you feel wonderful. This is a vague similarity to what is being described.

There is yet another wonderful surprise in the spiritual. The pleasure that we get from feeling the One who gives is infinitely greater than the pleasure we receive when we are just taking for ourselves. This is because the first kind of taking ties us with the Complete Giver, the Eternal One, the Creator.

But the soul does not start out being able to do this. The soul, a point in each of our hearts, begins as just a point, a desire to enjoy pleasure from the Creator. It develops into a "Vessel" to receive this pleasure. Kabbalah calls this Vessel a *Kli*. But at this initial state, it is only a mere desire to receive and is not considered a Vessel because it is unsuitable for reception.

Right now, we are as distanced from the Creator as we can be, enveloped in a hard casing of will to receive. As we currently exist, this concealment is not apparent to us as people. We go on about our business in this world. We work, eat, sleep, play, procreate, and experience our corporeal lives without any hint that there is anything else besides what we experience in this world. Yet for one whose point in the heart has awakened, and has crossed that barrier into the spiritual, it becomes immediately obvious what this "barrier" is blocking out, what it conceals.

After the awakening of this point in the heart, we discover it is only a Vessel for giving. A "giving Vessel" is one that still cannot receive for the purpose of pleasing the Creator, but can only refrain from receiving. It is in this state because if the Vessel would receive, it would be for itself. The soul can exist without receiving the Creator's Light because the sensation of shame caused by receiving for itself extinguishes its pleasure the moment it is received which turns the pleasure of reception into torment.

The solution that allows the soul to begin receiving at first seems ridiculous, almost backward. The soul discovers it must only receive pleasure as a *means to delight the Creator*. Let's repeat that. The soul must have such an attitude that it will not receive unless the act of its own reception brings pleasure to the Creator. Its own reception is no longer the driving force; it will only receive if the purpose of that act has nothing to do with itself, but only with the Creator. It is important that you understand we are speaking of spiritual pleasure here. The tiny drop of pleasure we experience in our world simply suffices to insure our existence, so live and enjoy.

The result of this discovery is actually a change in the soul's intent, from wanting to receive for itself to wanting to receive in order to bring pleasure to the Creator. In Kabbalah, this new and revolutionary intent is called a "screen." Only if there is a screen over the desire to enjoy (a willingness to take pleasure only to the extent that it delights the Creator), does the soul become worthy of reception. This point in the heart can then be called a "Vessel."

So all we really have to do is acquire a screen! It actually boils down to a change in our intent, from that of wanting to receive to that of wanting to give. But how does this screen work and how does it allow us to sense the Creator? The answer is simple; it works just like the rest of our senses.

For instance, let's take a look at the process of hearing. How do we hear? Air waves strike a kind of screen within our ear called an "eardrum." The eardrum is connected to specialized hearing organs that transfer the vibrations of the eardrum into electrical impulses that our brains interpret as sound.

The sense of sight is no different. Light strikes a kind of screen, the retina, where nerves are stimulated and transfer electric signals into the brain that it interprets as sight, what we see. If you remove either of the "screens" from these sensory organs, no matter how much air is moved in the form of sound waves, or how much light enters the eye, we still will not hear or see. Our other senses have the same types of screen mechanisms. The spiritual screen is no different. Light is reflected off the screen and signals are sent within us allowing us to sense the Creator.

Let's look at this process in spiritual terms. When the will to enjoy receives and feels the Giver as well, it feels both pleasure and shame. The shame happens because by receiving, the soul senses itself as opposite to the Creator. The presence of the Giver makes the receiver feel shame, and that shame stops us from enjoyment. In spirituality, when we receive, we feel we must give something back to the Giver, to equalize with the Giver so we do not feel as if we are only receiving.

Let's say that for years Betty and Bob have been going out to dinner every Friday night with another couple. But if Bob loses his job, he no longer has the money for this. When Bob calls the couple to tell them they cannot go out, as good friends they understand the situation and might talk Betty and Bob into letting them pick up the tab. Of course, Betty and Bob would still enjoy themselves, but perhaps not quite as much as they normally would. When that check is laid on the table, a disconcerting feeling arises.

But how about the next week when Bob is still unemployed? At some point, any of us would simply say "no thanks," mainly stemming from that feeling of shame, that feeling that we are not doing our part. We decline because this minute amount of shame would make us miserable.

Multiply that sense of shame several million times over and one begins to understand what kind of shame is involved with regard to taking pleasure from the Creator for one's own enjoyment while sensing Him. Our souls simply cannot do it.

One might ask, if the presence of the Creator can evoke such a sensation in us, how can we say that the decision is really for the Creator? So in order for us to make an independent decision to receive for the Creator and so we can come to resemble the One who created us in order to delight us, the Creator has to be concealed, just as He is to us today. That way our decision will not be compulsory, like not sticking our hands in fire because we know fire will burn.

We actually need the original concealment. It is our guarantee that until we are ready to receive only if it pleases Him, we cannot possibly do so. In order to give us that opportunity, there must be a situation where we creatures feel that we are the only ones here. Then, all the decisions will be our own.

The soul is not apparent or awake in us from the beginning. In each of us there is an "embryo" of a soul, but whether or not the soul has come to the point where it is ready to begin growing is a totally different story. If the soul has not yet come to that state, a person will not feel any desire for spirituality, for the Creator. But once the point in the heart begins to stir and demand, we begin to sense a faint question that turns into a desperate plea to know the purpose of our lives. This burning question becomes so intense that we finally reach a point where, without the answer to that question, we simply cannot go on living.

When we reach a stage where the point in the heart begins to stir, and we begin that process of revealing the Creator, we suddenly feel drawn to something exalted. That attraction is misinterpreted. Everyone feels this preliminary sensation, but after we experience that sensation several times, it diminishes because we learn correctly and begin to create within us those Vessels that will help us feel spiritual sensations.

We stop being like embryos in the womb and become more and more mature. Our emotions are then redefined and analyzed, and we grow farther away from our preliminary situation. Instead of wanting to be "enveloped" in something higher like an embryo, we begin aspiring to attain the Upper One Himself, to consciously wrap ourselves inside His attributes and try to move forward independently. That is possible only if we begin to acquire that spiritual Vessel for progress we call the "screen." That is exactly what Kabbalah teaches.

The soul only revokes its first restriction for one reason. What do we sense when we feel the Creator? We sense His intense desire to give, to delight us. If we do feel the desire of the Creator to please us, we can decide that despite the sensation of shame, we will accept the pleasure because that is what the Creator wants. Therefore, by doing so, we can bring pleasure to the Creator for His Sake, not for ourselves. The act remains as before, and we still receive just as we did when we felt shame, but the intent of our reception has now changed.

The decision has been taken only out of the desire to delight the Creator, despite the sensation of shame. But we as creatures discover that by acting for the Creator, we do not feel ourselves as receivers, but as givers. As creatures, through our equivalence of form with the Creator, we feel total wholeness, eternity, unending love and pleasure.

But the decision to restrict the reception of Light (the First Restriction), to receive Light only for the Creator, will come only if we feel the Creator, the Giver, because only the sensation of the Creator can awaken such a resolution in us. From that point forward, our advancement depends on us alone.

CHAPTER 5.
THE RESEARCH MATERIALS OF KABBALAH

Kabbalah has always been taught through books. The first books about Kabbalah were written thousands of years ago. Adam wrote the book, *Raziel Hamalaach* (*The Angel Raziel*), and Abraham the Patriarch wrote the book *Sefer Yetzira* (*Book of Creation*). The *Zohar* was written some 1900 years ago. All of these books are still available today.

The principal, fundamental book that we study is called *Talmud Eser Sefirot* (*The Study of the Ten Sefirot*). It consists of six volumes and more than 2000 pages that depict the laws of the system of creation in scientific terms. When we study them, we receive a special illumination, a special Providence from Above.

The reason for studying this great work is because it is written in a manner meant for people in this generation. Throughout history, Kabbalists have written materials that were meant for a specific generation. The materials from different generations actually provide the same material, but are presented in a manner that is easiest for that generation to understand.

But even if we still do not understand a single word we read, even if we haven't got a clue about the spiritual world, approaching the Creator begins from the very first lesson. When Kabbalists write books, they have already reached a certain spiritual level. When we read the books, wanting to somehow make contact with that world from which the Kabbalist wrote, we are enfolded in an illumination from that place. We do not feel it, but it slowly prepares us for the phase when we begin to feel more and more of what the books describe.

This is how one begins the process of entering the spiritual world. Of course, it is not as simple as presented here. For instance, at Bnei Baruch, there is a whole system that involves studying specific articles and lessons and following a specific syllabus.

In short, we have an entire system, the System of Creation awaiting us. The system of creation is everything around us: what is perceived, misperceived, and not perceived. Our emotions contain what we perceive by our five senses as well as something extra. That something extra is what we cannot feel today—a "sixth sense"—an additional sense that will be developed in us in the future. We call the information perceived in that sense, "The System of Creation."

The text in genuine books of Kabbalah precisely describes how the mechanism that operates reality works. Using charts and formulas, it depicts the "control room of reality" in a form much like a user's manual. These visuals teach us how the laws work in spirituality, and how we can influence them with mind and will, consequently affecting the results that will return to affect us.

THE ZOHAR

In Hebrew, Zohar means "splendor," as in: "The righteous sit with their crowns on their heads, and delight in the splendor of Divinity." The sensation of the Creator (the Light) in the collective soul is called "Divinity," according to The Zohar. In any place where the books of Kabbalah say, "So it was written in the book..." this always refers to The Zohar. All the others are seemingly not considered books because the word "book" (Sefer in Hebrew) comes from the word Sefira, which comes from the word "sapphire," radiance, a revelation (of the Light, the Creator). This is found only in The Zohar.

The Zohar is an important Kabbalistic book, but it is written in a concealed way, making it impossible to understand until a person has attained the spiritual world. Because of that, today we do not start with The Book of Zohar. Instead, there are introductions and books by Yehuda Ashlag (who is also known as Baal HaSulam) that teach us how to understand what is written in The Zohar.

The Book of Zohar is not a book through which one can attain spirituality; it was written for those who have already attained spirituality.

In order to understand it properly, we need to study several other books first, such as: The Science of Kabbalah, Introduction to The Book of Zohar, Preface to The Book of Zohar and Foreword to The Book of Zohar. Without first acquiring clear and correct knowledge through those introductions, the book will remain incomprehensible to us.

Baal HaSulam considers this question in the Introduction to The Book of Zohar (item 61): "We must also ask why was the commentary to The Zohar not revealed before the time of the Ari. Why was it not revealed to his predecessors? And most perplexing of all, why were the words of the Ari and the commentary to The Zohar not revealed until today?"

First, why was The Zohar hidden? The answer is that the world has gone through three phases of development during its 6000 years of existence. The first 2000 are called Tohu, the middle 2000, Torah, and the last 2000, The Days of the Messiah. It is important to note here that the 6,000 years of existence have nothing to do with the age of the world. They pertain to the period during which humans have been spiritually evolving.

During the first 2000 years, the souls that descended were sublime souls with small desires and small Lights. Desire was pretty much limited to physical existence. They were not even given the Torah because for these souls, simply existing was enough to correct them.

In the next 2000 years, souls descended with more evolved desires that needed a greater Light for their correction, the Light of the Torah. Toward the end of the 6000 years, in the remaining third, the coarsest souls descend. Those souls need the greatest Lights for their correction - the Light of the Kabbalah. Kabbalah was not needed prior to that, just as the Torah was not needed in the first two thousand years.

During the time of the Ari (end of the 16th century), we grew closer to the end of the correction of the main part, the third and last phase of the development of the souls. As a result, the sublime wisdom was revealed through the soul of the Ari. The souls of the first generations were higher than those of the last, but the greater the correction that is needed, the greater the consequent attainment and adhesion to the Creator.

During the last 2000 years, especially from the time of the Ari, the souls that descend to this world become increasingly coarser and more egotistical. They must therefore study and implement Kabbalah for their correction. This is easy to see, as today our desires run rampant even compared to just a few hundred years ago.

The Zohar was written as it was on purpose, as the book itself will tell you. Only those who have already grasped the spiritual reality can know what is written there and see the text as a depiction of spiritual situations. They see the pictures and identify the spiritual states they pertain to. We cannot do that because we still don't have the spiritual vision.

The writings of the Ari, however, aim at more developed souls from later cycles, and therefore appear different to us. But the most suitable for us are the writings of Yehuda Ashlag, Baal HaSulam. These are intended for our generation, which is why they appear to us as systematic textbooks, just as for any science, much like the texts we study at a university. They offer questions and answers, interpretations of the meaning of the words, and a clear division of issues, which differ by topic. They also show how to perform the relevant topic of discussion. There are special articles that go along with these books that specify how one should personally relate to one's study.

Our generation has no problem approaching the immediate study of Kabbalah. Unlike all other sciences, this wisdom demands no prior study. It is enough for a person to feel that life is difficult, to have a sense of restlessness, to see life as meaningless, or to just begin to question the meaning of life. Then, one can start studying the books and begin to advance.

In the second item in his Introduction to *The Study of the Ten Sefirot*, the most complex text in the study of Kabbalah, Baal HaSulam specifies the person to whom he is writing the book. He aims it at only those who feel the burning question, "What is the meaning of my life?"

He adds further in item 155 that by studying, even though the student does not understand the content of the book, the text will reveal to the student ways to behave in order to attain spirituality.

THE STUDY OF THE TEN SEFIROT

The book, *Shaar HaGilgulim*, describes how the Ari at his deathbed forbade all his disciples except Chaim Vital to study Kabbalah. Chaim Vital did not fully attain Kabbalah at that time, and therefore decided not to edit or publish the writings of the Ari.

Three generations later, Rav Tzemach, Rav Paprish and Chaim Vital's son, Shmuel, began to dig out the Ari's writings little by little, sort them out and publish them in book form. However, none of them possessed the entire collection, and therefore could not correctly understand and compile the Ari's system of Kabbalah.

Only in *The Study of the Ten Sefirot* was the system rendered complete. For that reason, we do not study the other books that Rav Tzemach, Rav Paprish, and Shmuel Vital published, although we sometimes take an excerpt from them, as was done by Baal HaSulam in *The Study of the Ten Sefirot*. Besides *The Study of the Ten Sefirot*, no other books (here I don't mean articles and letters on the spiritual work) contain any systematic compilation of the science of Kabbalah.

CHAPTER 6.
STUDYING KABBALAH

The importance of studying this wondrous wisdom is that there is a great power in the study of Kabbalah that can be of benefit to everyone. The soul starts its existence in the world of *Ein Sof* (lit. No End). It then descends through five levels of concealment Kabbalah refers to as "Higher Worlds," before finally clothing our physical bodies. The names of this system of higher worlds are: *Adam Kadmon, Atzilut, Beria, Yetzira,* and *Assiya*.

The principal law of the Higher Worlds is altruism. This law acts whether we are aware of it or not, and we must follow it whether we like it or not. Disobeying that law produces disasters and tragedies, both individual and collective. That law is not canceled, although we are stopped as soon as we break it. We will only be able to understand when and how that law works by studying the wisdom of Kabbalah.

The result of our descent into this world is that we are completely dependent on the components and characteristics of that spiritual system. So in order to function according to its laws, we must study that system instead of roaming blindly through our world, beaten time and again but not knowing why. When we study Kabbalah, even if we do not understand anything we study, but simply have the desire to understand, we awaken within us an influence of the Light that corrects us. It is the soul's need to reclaim the Light that filled it before it came down to our world.

Who can study this wisdom? Anyone who relentlessly asks, "What is the meaning of my life?" can study Kabbalah. This great wisdom can only be studied when there is an inner need, not through coercion. When Rav Kook was asked who was permitted to study Kabbalah, he replied: "Anyone who wants to." If a person really wants to study, it is a sign that he or she is ready.

When a person truly wants something, that person goes out and does it. Therefore, if your soul is ready for ascension, you'll study Kabbalah. And if your soul is not yet ready, you'll remain for awhile on the outskirts of Kabbalah. After some time, you'll drift away from it and go on ripening elsewhere. Keep in mind that you do not find Kabbalah on your own; you are brought here from Above.

Bans regarding the study of the Kabbalah existed only until the time of the Ari. Kabbalists themselves enforced them because the souls did not yet need the Kabbalah to progress toward the purpose of creation. But since the time of the Ari (end of the 16th century), he and other Kabbalists have lifted the ban they had set up. It was done because souls have reached such a level of development that they've begun to feel within them the need for spiritual, exalted content.

If earlier people were still passive in the process, now we are compelled to partake in the process. The only condition is that we show a desire to partake in the leadership. Otherwise, the Spiritual Force will force us to want it. There is not a quiet place left on earth. No one will be calm anywhere, especially those with a point in the heart, because the Spiritual Law that takes us to the center of creation affects those people first.

We should use the very means that we were born with to approach the Creator and to believe that in each given moment the means that are at our disposal are the very best there are. Despite that, we must never stop searching for better ones. Kabbalah is an understanding of the Creator, of the purpose of creation, a revelation of the Upper Light (within you, in your emotions), by changing your intentions. It is much like the Bible, in the sense that it, too, is not a historical tale, but a description of the universe and a method to understand the Creator.

In Kabbalah, the term "forbidden" actually means, "it cannot be done." For example, when it was said that it is forbidden to see the Creator, it means that it is forbidden to receive Light in order to please yourself. Therefore, the words, "forbidden to study Kabbalah" actually mean, "It cannot be studied because of a lack of will." The statement is still correct today as far as the general public is concerned, but the souls that descend to our world today will reach such a level of spiritual development that all their thoughts and earthly desires will become their aspirations for their Creator.

No secrets are taught in Kabbalah. The wisdom of Kabbalah is called "the wisdom of the hidden," not because it is secret in and of itself, but because it reveals things that were hidden before we began to study. It reveals everything that surrounds us.

However, the wisdom of Kabbalah is comprised of two parts: "flavors of the Torah" and "secrets of the Torah." The flavors of the Torah investigate the structure of the spiritual worlds, the soul, and how one should correct oneself. Everyone is permitted to study that part. This material is described in books of Kabbalah, sold all over the world, and translated into English, Russian, and many other languages. Anyone can taste the flavors of the Torah.

The "secrets of the Torah" are the hidden part of the Torah. Nothing is written about this in any book. That part is taught only after a person has acquired the flavors of the Torah, attained the structure of the spiritual worlds, as well as one's own spiritual structure. A person who has attained that level, where physical life and death do not exist, sees the entire process from beginning to end and is above our world. Then the secrets open up like innermost fountains, and we understand the rudimentary laws of that system.

People often ask if there is a prerequisite to studying Kabbalah. The simple answer is that you don't have to study anything before you begin to study Kabbalah, because Kabbalah is *contact with the Creator*. A person who wants to study Kabbalah is like an infant emerging wet and naked from its mother's womb. What would an infant need to know at that point? When we want to learn about the Upper World, we do not need anything that we learned in this world, because it is the Upper World we wish to enter. In order to be interested in Kabbalah, you don't need any preconditions other than finding the right sources of information.

Our genuine development from matter to spirit should evolve gradually, to the extent that we understand the world we live in. The more we discover the true situation in our world, the more we will be ready for an inner change. The law of the Upper World defines it in the words: "There is no coercion in spirituality." Only the Creator can change our desires and intentions, so if we study diligently, the change will come.

We move through our world totally oblivious that anything outside of our perceived reality exists until we decide to study Kabbalah and attain the necessary knowledge to understand and work with the system of creation. This is regarded as the highest degree, the last degree that any person, any soul can and eventually must attain. The method of Kabbalah prepares us to enter the Upper World with knowledge and powers, without harming ourselves or others. We enter the spiritual world only by the extent of our correction. Consequently, there cannot be a situation where a person enters prematurely and inflicts damage. The measure of our correction is the measure of our penetration to the Upper World, as well as the degree of cooperation with Providence.

Kabbalah is a very real and accurate system by which we begin to gradually feel the Creator in mind and heart, to an even greater extent than we feel our current environment. The Creator is sensed a lot more clearly, without any self-deception, and through controlled and systematically repeated actions. This wisdom is subject to all the requirements that exact sciences are subject to. We can measure emotions and translate them to numbers; we can also conduct experiments, repeat them and transfer the acquired knowledge to others. Because of all that, Kabbalah is regarded as a science.

We use everything we're given in this world freely. We do not feel where and from whom it comes. If we were to feel the Giver, even slightly, we would instantly receive a different sensation, a different position, and a different relationship with anything or anyone. That would immediately place us in a completely different situation. Our whole problem is the absence of the sensation of the Creator. That is why the single most important goal in our world is to feel the existence of the Creator, to establish some sort of contact with Him.

After that, contact will become much easier. When you attain even a little bit of the sensation of the Creator, you hang on to it, and can return again and again to deepen and broaden it. Once you have achieved the ability to turn to the Creator, you can comprehend the kind of response you will get. This is what is meant by the phrase, "One's soul tutors one." This means that one is led by one's own soul. Our own feelings tell us how we should proceed.

Many people try to deter others from Kabbalah: they can be religious, secular, strangers and relatives. I tried to fight the craving to know the purpose of my life, and I couldn't picture a day when I could get up in the morning without asking the same haunting question over and over again. I couldn't imagine a peaceful, thought-free day, where I could sit down quietly and enjoy my life.

If there's no cure for it, it's like a curse. But the cure exists. If you feel that question burning in your gut, leaving you restless, you might be losing precious time listening to the advice of others and living by their reason, because ultimately you'll go back to what your soul craves.

It is written, "One learns from one's soul," so listen to yourself and you'll know what it is you want. If you can rise above the level of those who advise against study, there is nothing that can stop you. Sooner or later you'll come to Kabbalah.

Often, people want to know how long a course in Kabbalah is or exactly how long this process takes. Today's society would prefer everything boxed and ready to be picked up. But attaining spiritual wisdom requires a bit more effort. The wisdom of Kabbalah is a science and a way of life that enables us to live correctly. How long does it take to learn how to live correctly? That depends on the soul. But when we begin to study, we soon feel that we can no longer do without it, because life without our studies is so strange and narrow that without connecting life to the Upper World, to the soul, and to eternity, it loses its meaning. When we begin to feel like that, it is no longer possible to detach ourselves from Kabbalah and remain confined to our world.

Nowadays, we also run into a lot of different systems calling themselves Kabbalah. Generally speaking, there were two systems in the study of Kabbalah: one was called the "Kabbalah of the RAMAK" (Rav Moshe Kordoviro); the other is the "Kabbalah of the Ari." The first was in use until the 16th century, when at the beginning of that century, the Kabbalah of the Ari was established. The Ari described it in his books, and all the Kabbalists after him followed in his footsteps. Baal HaSulam, under whose writings we study, is strictly a Kabbalist of the system of the Ari known as "Lurianic Kabbalah."

The souls that descended to our world before the Ari were from the "old type." But from his time on, there was a drastic change in the souls that descended, and some of them began to demand spiritual elevation. In modern times, many people think Kabbalah is only studied by those who are Jewish (meaning those following the ways of Judaism). Kabbalah is a method for connecting with the Creator, who is unique. In Kabbalah, a gentile who progresses toward the Creator is called "Jewish," and a Jew who doesn't is called a "gentile."

It is also important to note that there is no age limit for the study of Kabbalah. Bnei Baruch has a student who is eighty years old, and also has students who have not finished high school. When you study, there are no differences between age or origin. The soul doesn't make such distinctions.

Kabbalah is almost always studied in groups, over the internet, in local groups, and even some international groups exist. A group study accelerates the spiritual progress of a person who studies alone millions of times over. One who studies alone can only use one's own Vessel to receive the Light of the Creator, meaning spirituality.

People who study in a group create a kind of spiritual Vessel that consists of all the participants, and everyone begins to enjoy the group's illumination. Let us assume that there are ten participants. The illumination that is received is not ten times as much as a single individual can receive, but millions of times stronger. The reason is the incorporation, meaning the soul of each and every one of the participants consists of 620 parts, with each part joining the others. The mixture of the parts together creates one collective Vessel.

Even more important, the group must have a teacher. Studying without a teacher is impossible. The teacher should explain about the spiritual structure, how it works, how to approach it and how to raise oneself to it. Teachers should also explain how we can lift ourselves to a higher spiritual degree and how to control that spiritual level. There has almost never been a case in history when someone rose without assistance. It was almost always a case of a teacher and a student working together.

Dr. Laitman is often asked, "How can you prove to me that you are the teacher I need?" This is a very good and just question. Dr. Laitman usually answers in the following way: "It is your life. It was given to you just once and you want to make the most of it. But how can a teacher prove to you that they are better than anybody else?"

Kabbalah has a very simple answer: one should study where one's heart desires, where one feels one belongs. It should not be a place where you are being persuaded to feel that it's "your place," or that you're being pushed to accept. When you detach yourself from persuasions, from anything external, from your upbringing and from everything that you have heard in your entire life, and feel in your heart that it is the place for you, then you should stay. That is the only test!

To correct another fallacy, there is also no discrimination regarding whether men or women can study Kabbalah. Both sexes must develop spiritually. The only difference lies in the method. The beginning of the learning process is the same. That is why in our introductory courses there is no difference between the method provided for men and for women.

Later on, if a person goes deeper into the study of the actual Kabbalah, the difference in the method becomes apparent. Men and women begin to perceive the world differently, because men and women are indeed two different worlds and have a different perception of creation. In point of fact, the souls of men are more corrupt and need more correction than those of women. Sorry, guys!!!!

CHAPTER 7.
THE STUDY METHOD OF KABBALAH

Once you have recognized that burning question within you that demands you seek answers, you must also have an initial desire for the Creator. If it's there, you need nothing more! If you have been endowed with such a desire, the whole process is in your hands from that moment on, because all the forces you need are already in your soul. All it takes is to develop them, and that's your work. It is in your power to do so because your unique body was created specifically to allow you to attain the purpose of creation. Therefore, no one can say that they were incapable, that circumstances prevented them from attaining the goal for which they were born in this world.

If you're in the initial stages of your studies, you should read a lot, but only what you can understand. Read a lot and don't stop. Avoid difficult parts because what you can understand easily now will help you later to understand the harder parts.

The learning material in Kabbalah is divided into two parts:

1. A study of the creation of the worlds, the *Partzufim* and the *Sefirot*, the concatenation of the degrees of the concealment of the Creator. That part is crucial to our understanding of the system of creation and its activity. It is studied in the following order: Preface to the Wisdom of the Kabbalah, *The Study of the Ten Sefirot*, selected sections of *The Zohar* and *The Tree of Life*. This material must be studied systematically.

2. The ascent of the soul through the degrees of the Spiritual Worlds from below upward. A student must read and reread freely the parts that are of most interest. These are studied through the articles and the letters. They were not written in the same language as *The Study of the Ten Sefirot*, but in the language of emotion, ethics, analysis of actions and so on. It is not really the wisdom of Kabbalah, but how it is used for the ascent of the soul. You'll read about it in the books of Baal HaSulam and Rabash, as well as in Dr. Michael Laitman's books. The study is

comprised of an acquaintance with the material, meaning a systematic scan of the material in order to be able to find references. This is done because people who study Kabbalah so they will ascend spiritually are under perpetual changes, and must pick the material they read according to the state they're in at that moment.

Thousands of books have been written throughout the history of Kabbalah, but the instructions of Rabash were to study only through these sources:

- The writings of Rav Shimon Bar-Yochai
- The writings of the Ari
- The writings of Baal HaSulam

I suggest new students to start with studying these sources. Later on, when you have absorbed the material, you'll be able to understand other writers. This will give you a solid basis from which to examine other sources to see if they suit you as well.

At Bnei Baruch, beginners are strongly recommended to use only a number of selected sources. This is because, although everything in the world does point to the Creator, we are unable to see it. In order to see, we must know the right direction, have a correct approach to reality, and learn the fundamentals of the Universal Design and the rules of its development, its goal, and the limitations of our perception.

It is important to note that by no means do we devalue other sources. Many Kabbalists were at an even higher degree than Rav Shimon Bar-Yochai or the Ari. However, they were not permitted to write, or if they were permitted, it was with minor implications that were meant for those who were already in the Upper Worlds.

The articles we study rely a great deal on the Ladder commentary. Rav Yehuda Ashlag (Baal HaSulam) named his commentaries on *The Zohar HaSulam* (The Ladder), because reading it helps us in our world climb the ladder toward the Creator, spanning every degree in between. That is the purpose of creation. Note that *The Zohar* commentaries can be understood only after studying all its introductions.

Some do study Kabbalah for the knowledge alone. To aspire simply to "know" is wonderful, although it mustn't be an aspiration for knowledge alone, but rather for attainment: in order to attain the studied material from within you, to discover who your "self" is and where within you lies the subject matter the books describe. After all, everything that's written there is written from within, from the writers' personal attainment.

No reasoning in the world will help us understand spirituality because it is above our reason and our minds. This is why we can't feel it. Our senses can only examine things they can grasp and analyze, a knowledge that we generally refer to as "this world." In order to feel the Upper World we must acquire other senses, which we call a "screen." Only with a screen can we feel what is above us, beyond our material sensations, which our natural senses cannot detect. When we are able to sense the Upper World, we also receive a different mind and a different reason.

First, we get the wisdom and the reason of the Upper World. Then, we begin to feel it. The only way to acquire a screen is through the wisdom of Kabbalah.

Therefore, when we read books about Kabbalah, the authors speak to us from exactly the degree they are describing. There is no time in spirituality. As the greatest Kabbalist of our time, Rav Yehuda Ashlag says, "...but out of the great desire and yearning to understand what they are learning, they awaken upon themselves the lights that surround their souls" (Introduction to *The Study of the Ten Sefirot*, item 155).

Out of a great desire to attain what they are studying, the readers awaken in themselves a surrounding Light from the same spiritual degrees they're reading about. What is important is the intent. But the problem is that we cannot force the right intent on ourselves. That aim should come from the heart, provided the heart really wants it. This will occur if there is a need to attain something higher, if our souls have developed to the point where they need the Creator, not the material things in this world.

Sometimes we simply do not feel like studying. But in fact, it's actually good to study when you feel you're not in the mood for it. At such times, it is best to study the structure of the worlds. There can be great benefits to studying "against yourself," and against your current mood.

For example, if I'm in despair, I should read articles about yearning for the Creator. We have to experience all the emotions. After all, we are built from combinations of all the feelings and attributes that exist in the world. In Kabbalah you experiment on yourself.

Only the soul can sense its true desires. We ourselves do not feel them. We may think that a certain desire is burning within, and may actually be deluding ourselves. Yet the soul is what will finally lead us to our goal, as it has led us thus far. It is not through our wisdom or conscious thought that we have come to aspire to the Upper Light.

In order to develop the necessary attributes for growth within, it is advised that "Whatsoever thy hand attaineth to do by thy strength, that do." This means that you should do everything you can to absorb as much material as possible. Read, even if only to enrich your knowledge and brag to your friends about it. In time, the sheer quantity of your studies will bear fruit.

This is also true regarding the first stage of your studies. In order to absorb as much information as possible, it is acceptable to lie to yourself and set goals, specifying self-benefit. But afterwards you will realize that your results depend on the quality of the material, meaning your approach and your intentions. That is why it says, "The Light in it reforms." The proper intention is what leads us to attainment.

Anything we attain and speak of is what we attain within ourselves. What we hear, see and feel are not external objects, but our own responses to those objects. When we attain the Creator, we realize that nothing really changes outside us. Only we change inwardly, and we relate to those inner changes as if they were external ones.

People make every effort to absorb everything around them and take in as much as they can with as little effort as possible. In such a state, as complete egoists, we experience only our internal responses. But when we succeed in restricting our intentions to please ourselves, we begin to want to please the Creator, to feel what is outside us, namely the Creator, without aiming for ourselves.

Then, to the extent that we want "not for ourselves," we feel the Light of the Creator. To the extent that we get to know the Creator, we feel a desire to give to Him, which results in the buildup of a reciprocal bond between us and the Creator. This extent of the revelation of the Creator is called a "degree." In our emotions, these degrees are organized in five groups called "worlds." These are the measurements of the discovery and concealment of the Creator.

Sometimes when studying the system of the worlds, students get to the point of the creation of *Malchut* and the first restriction. After that, they stop understanding and can't make any more progress. It is actually a good sign if you cannot understand the simplest things. It means that your soul demands to be filled with the sensation of the Creator. This suppresses the need for intellectual understanding. As a result, you do not fill up your brain because your soul will not let you!

However, without a screen, the soul cannot be filled up, either. As a result, one tries to learn but can't understand anything. In fact, this is another good sign that shows one's inner demand for spiritual development.

Those whose souls do not motivate them toward inner sensations, but toward knowledge, will study well and gain a tremendous amount of knowledge. However, their souls will remain empty. At the same time, their knowledge is revealed to be shallow; they don't understand the inner processes because the Creator made a Vessel of desire, not a Vessel of understanding, so knowledge of Kabbalah can arise only from emotional scrutiny.

In the Introduction to *The Study of the Ten Sefirot*, Rav Yehuda Ashlag writes that, unlike a business that demands skills, memory, technical abilities, agility, rhythmic sense, and strength, the study of Kabbalah demands no skills, because all the skills are attributes of the body that is in this world. In other words, these attributes pertain to the nature of this world, which are not involved in attaining the Upper One.

People often wonder if, by studying Kabbalah, they will become smarter. A person's desires are very small at birth. Then they begin to develop to a slight degree. How much these desires develop determines how much the mind develops. The brain can develop only to the extent that it must in order to satisfy our desires. But when we embark on the study of Kabbalah, our desires grow and we become more and more egotistical, and therefore smarter. But there is no need to worry: when you study, you will get everything you need for your development from Above. You will actually feel something new within you—a gift from the Creator.

Sometimes after years of studying Kabbalah, the goal of one's life becomes "routine." Those special thoughts seem to disappear, and it sometimes feels as if there is no movement or attainment. Sometimes the goal itself disappears. This is, in fact, temporary. It is when we feel absolute emptiness, which occurs only when we strive for attainment with all our might, that we make real progress.

Our struggle may be made under the most desperate of situations and after years of disappointments and the perpetual reawakening of our aspirations towards our goal. Then, gradually, it becomes clear that only the Creator can change our situations. Such change can occur only by our total devotion, despite the fact that the shells, meaning our egoistic desires to enjoy the Light of the Creator, constantly tell us that we can still do things by ourselves. Only then, and without any warning, comes the help of the Creator, like a dream come true, at the least expected moment.

The most important thing in Kabbalah is to attain the screen that you begin cultivating on your own. The screen is born and develops in us without any intent on our part, because we don't know what it is. All the new things that appear in us are solely the direct result of our studies.

We cannot know what will appear in us the next minute. It will always be something new and unfamiliar, so how can we know about it in advance? How can we anticipate it?

"New" means something from a higher degree than my current one. Therefore a screen cannot be cultivated intentionally.

If after awhile you lack joy from your study environment, remember that it is a temporary state. Keep studying and your alienation from society will soon be replaced by the opposite situation: you'll feel that there are more pleasures around you than you ever felt before. Then, you'll discover within you a greater will to receive than before. This will happen to give you something to correct.

When you feel a lack of desire for the spiritual hits, read a lot, and read only the material that your teacher suggests, those parts that your heart desires. At times such as these, my teacher suggested I divide the study between the Preface to the Wisdom of Kabbalah and articles and letters. Study whichever calls to your soul.

Moods often change along the way. This is natural and shows you're making progress. The articles you'll read will show you that your feelings and thoughts are typical of one who is making progress. In the morning, before work, study in The Science of Kabbalah for an hour, and before you go to bed read the letters and articles that speak of inner work.

When you, as a student of Kabbalah, feel a lack of excitement, what you are feeling is the beginning of your receiving new values and your reaction to this phenomenon. This period takes some time; you cannot perform significant changes all at once because your mind, your fundamental systems, your nervous system, and the reciprocal relationships with your environment make it very difficult for you to do so.

If you experience this, the good news is that you have already begun the initial process of inner change. Keep studying and asking questions. You're just like any other person who feels the initial effects of correct study on your inner world. A person who studies Kabbalah does not descend from a previous state, but climbs to a higher one, so there's no reason for despair, much less depression.

There's a law in nature called "the law of equivalence of form." That law makes objects with similar attributes draw nearer, and objects with opposite attributes distance themselves from each other. When signs of spiritual attributes arise, that law begins to act on us to the degree that we have attained these attributes. If you study the material correctly, you'll soon find that many tiny changes happen within you. You'll find you are being led, that there's a soul within you, and that something is affecting it from the outside.

You'll find that your soul and the Light of the Creator, which affects it, are leading you, not your physical brain. Your mind contains knowledge of the present, whereas the future remains unknown. But even before the future is revealed to you, you want to do more than just fantasize about it; you want to act as if you are in it, as if you have risen to the next degree of awareness.

Sometimes after studying for awhile, a person may wish to drop certain things in their life and devote more time to their spiritual work. But externally, you must continue to work and not change a thing! No matter how much your interest drops, you must not follow your desires, but your duty.

When we study Kabbalah correctly, the surrounding Light that is awakened works our souls and initiates the next spiritual state. That state will arrive by itself and replace the present state. By making considerable efforts in the study of Kabbalah, a person can accelerate personal changes. That, in fact, is the only freedom of choice we have in this world.

Baal HaSulam writes in the Introduction to *The Study of the Ten Sefirot* that the Creator rests one's hand on good fortune and tells him: "Choose this for yourself." So where, then, is the choice? The choice is, in fact, that either we are pushed from behind, which we will feel as pain, or we run forward by ourselves, ahead of the pain. This is our only freedom of choice.

Anything that happens in our world, anything that people do, is all predetermined, because all our characteristics and our environment, both internal and external, are predefined by the Creator. Freedom of choice exists only for those who crave spirituality and only by their personal efforts.

Every student wants to know how to accelerate his or her spiritual progress and in so doing, avoid the agony. You can do this in the following ways:

• Read the books of Baal HaSulam, Rabash, and Dr. Laitman.

• Join a group that aims to discover the objective of creation. Be active and do things for the members of the group and the spiritual leader.

• Begin to write everything you know about spirituality. That way, you can correct your current spiritual degree more quickly and create a need to attain the next degree.

• Take an active part in circulating the wisdom of the Kabbalah. This is the most effective means of all.

People often have questions about so called "bad situations." Actually, from a Kabbalistic point of view, bad situations do not exist. The Creator gives us everything for the sole purpose of correcting us. There is the Creator, there is us and there is what we receive from Him.

It is said "The Light of the Creator makes one weary." The Light shows us who and what we are, that we're only tiny egoists. However, it shows us our weaknesses—our enslavement to our ego—only to the degree that we can bear what we see. The more we develop and correct, the more obvious it becomes that we are lowly, and far different from the Creator. We are shown this to correct ourselves by simply recognizing our own nature, and then rejecting it. Each time we read the right books, we will realize more and more deeply who we are and who the Creator is.

What is the meaning of the study of Kabbalah? When we begin our studies, according to our progress in life, we begin to aim our actions toward the goal, which is to attain a spiritual contact with the Creator. We go under His private Providence exactly to that extent, which is the purpose of our search, though our search is still an unconscious one.

If we read only genuine books about the spiritual world, if that is what we find interesting, we are already under the private Providence of the Creator. The Creator guides everyone, but He guides us personally. Every soul receives the Light from Above with growing intensity, and therefore develops in accordance with the purpose of creation. This is called "general Providence." But when He takes us out of the ranks to promote us faster and pull us toward Him, it is called "private Providence."

In a state of Private Providence, we begin to feel ups and downs. These will be expressed in our sensation of the Creator or its absence, according to our own attributes. We will stop looking at life as others do. While others say, "Thank God another day went by. I stayed healthy, I did a few things," we, on the other hand, will start evaluating ourselves in greater detail.

We will ask ourselves, "Am I closer to the Creator today? Do I have a desire for Him?" Even if our answers are negative, they are nonetheless a testimony to our progress.

Contrary to all religions and philosophies, Kabbalah states clearly and unequivocally that spiritual ascent means increased pleasure. The beginning of the path includes the study of the Kabbalah, while the reader maintains a regular way of life without change or limitations. But since our desires influence our acts, if we want to achieve something sublime, we must act accordingly.

Thus, we see that the correction is a process involving the effect of the Upper Light on us. It is not a process of restriction by coercion. That is precisely the difference between Kabbalah and religion: Kabbalah activates the power of the Creator— it is not an oppressing force from the outside. Therefore, when we receive more and more strength from Above, it opens up the channels for greater desires, which can then be corrected and used appropriately.

We cannot live without pleasure. After all, our very essence is the will to receive delight and pleasure, and the purpose of creation is the attainment of perfect pleasure. There's nothing wrong with the pleasure itself; we must correct its objective, not the desire itself. So what do I do with my desires? I want a big, beautiful house; though a small one will do just fine. I want a new car, though the old one still runs. As for my job, I'm still interested in one that bears more responsibility. Do I have to clear out these desires in order to make room for more study?

Anything in our lives—our choices, the steps we take, our preferences, and the way we evaluate our lives—is defined by how necessary we feel these things are. It is said that "All that a man hath will he give for his life" (Job 2:4). On the one hand, this quote can be interpreted this way: a person would sacrifice everything for life, health and the possibility to go on living. On the other hand, you can say that one would give everything away (life included) for something without which one's life would be pointless. We can find examples of this throughout history. Even in our materialistic time, everything depends on our appreciation of both material and spiritual values. These values change with our development, making self-coercion unnecessary.

In the Introduction to *The Study of the Ten Sefirot*, Rav Yehuda Ashlag explains that in the past, at the dawn of history, one who wanted to study Kabbalah and be introduced to spirituality had to restrict oneself and live on meager bread and water. But today, after corrections have been made in the world by more recent Kabbalists, along with the development of the souls from generation to generation, all it takes to reach the Upper World is the study of Kabbalah.

Therefore, the asceticism and restrictions that people used to practice are no longer necessary today. Kabbalists have drawn the Upper Light toward us, especially since the time of the Ari (16th century). As it says, "The Light in it reforms," meaning the study of Kabbalah awakens an invisible illumination of Upper Light that corrects us.

Kabbalists explain that the study of Kabbalah awakens this illumination within the disciple more intensively than does any other study. Therefore, they advise anyone who wants to attain spirituality and the purpose of creation to study Kabbalah. Of course you can go on building houses, buying cars and giving expensive gifts, but it's important to maintain regular studies, read any time you can, and read only the writings of genuine Kabbalists. That study will bring you new internal situations and new values by which you'll make your future decisions.

The primary and the secondary interests in your life will gradually change, but this change must come from within you, not by coercion. There should be no coercion in spirituality, and the source of the coercion in our world is the shells. The answer is to keep studying Kabbalah and be yourself at all times. In time, your soul will guide you and tell you how much energy to put into spirituality and how much to expend on activities in this world.

When we begin to study, sometimes we feel miserable because we don't know how to change our aim. I have no clue how to invert this, so that none of the things I do will be for my personal gain. Such feelings are good at the beginning of our studies. They show that we're progressing toward spirituality, toward the barrier, toward the sensations of the Upper World.

Each degree, each spiritual situation we experience, must die or disappear. In other words, we must discard the previous degree of growth as unworthy of our new state. The same applies to souls: new life begins only after death has occurred and the process of decay is completed.

Therefore, our current situation ends when it becomes intolerable. The desire to move on to the next phase is formed out of the intolerable present state. Disagreement with the present situation brings with it a new situation. Therefore, our solution lies in focusing solely on the quantity and the quality of our studies. We should read a lot (quantity) with the thought that each and every word should bring us new powers and change us from within (quality).

Only those who discover the Light in the Kabbalah find that their strength grows weaker. This is because they study it to receive strength from Above, to be corrected, and to resemble the Creator. They do not want to stay at the level of simply satisfying their bodily needs. As our sages say, "You are called man, and not those who commit idolatry."

Those who commit idolatry are those who worship their evil inclinations and bow before their egos. You can either bow before the Creator, or before your ego, because only those two possibilities exist. Bowing before something indicates the desire for it, or for the attribute it symbolizes. Bowing before the ego means a person places the ego above self; there is no desire to suppress it, but to feed on it. The surrender to the ego is called "bowing before an alien god." In the Kabbalah, this is called, "idolatry."

If the student studies Kabbalah in order to become a "human," the evil inclination sees that it has nothing to look for here and the natural forces weaken. But at that time, the person still does not have the spiritual powers of bestowal, and therefore is still not attracted to the Creator, as there is not yet the knowledge of who He is.

Being between the two worlds is the state that causes the indifference. It is a necessary phase. After that phase, the Creator gradually appears. Higher spiritual goals appear and the person moves on. If a student has fatigue that stems from the lack of genuine desire for spirituality, it is important to understand that there is a work, *Lo Lishma* (not for Her name - not for the Creator) and *Lishma* (for Her name - for the Creator). Working *Lo Lishma* is spiritual work that first entails working with the intent for self. In order to understand that you're working *Lo Lishma* (and not everyone attains even that), you feel at least slightly—as though from afar—the meaning of working *Lishma*, so that you can compare the two and realize that you're working *Lo Lishma*.

Yet, these are only mechanical acts. We must not delude ourselves that we have reached anything substantial. Then, gradually, we must ask the Creator to plant in us the power to perform a genuine spiritual act, just for Him. All of this happens gradually. A temporary physical weakness is a result of the passage from doing things for oneself, to doing them for the Creator.

Sometimes, we have a strong desire to share some of our newly acquired feelings with a friend. Students should never share inner sensations and emotions with anyone except the Creator or their teacher. That is because other people, even unintentionally, will project their egos onto us, and we will lose our mental strength for some time. Although we might feel temporary relief, we will temporarily lose the ability to climb to a higher degree when we share our feelings.

It is a very natural thing for us to speak only from ourselves. However, in our words, we always include our egos. It doesn't matter if the ego is concealed or revealed—the most important thing is not to talk about our spiritual feelings toward the Creator. We can talk about *Sefirot*, *Partzufim* and about the wisdom of Kabbalah indefinitely, as long as we don't show our feelings, because in doing so, we can harm both ourselves and our friends. The same applies to our spouses, children, and even complete strangers. Study the books, but never talk about your feelings.

The study of Kabbalah does not just include work in the books. Physical actions for the benefit of the group, organizing lectures and Kabbalah study groups are more beneficial than the study itself. Serving the teacher is also more beneficial than studying with him. In his Speech for the Completion of *The Zohar*, Rav Yehuda Ashlag quotes the following saying of ancient Kabbalist sages: "Make for yourself a rav and buy yourself a friend."

In other words, choose a person whom you think is important and make that person your teacher. Then, try to please him or her. Your teacher is very important to you. By pleasing your teacher, you'll get used to doing for others, and by the force of habit you'll be able to do the same for the Creator. By being spiritually close to your teacher, you'll receive the degree by which the teacher appreciates the Creator. That will give you a chance to do at least something for the Creator, and enter the spiritual world this way. At the same time, you will acquire the sensation of the greatness of the Creator and you'll be able to advance to complete adhesion with Him.

Observing your teacher's requests with the aim to fulfill them allows you to attain spiritual resemblance with them. You'll be able to receive their thoughts and knowledge, and above all, attain their love and attraction for the Creator, which would give you the ability to develop and progress spiritually. However, studying with your teacher is always motivated by the desire to attain personal knowledge for yourself. As a result, the study does not bring with it spiritual nearness to the Creator. In other words, by doing things for the teacher, you attain their thoughts and by studying you will attain only their words.

You can only attain their thoughts if the motivation to serve the teacher stems from the desire to please the teacher, and not yourself. In the opposite situation, when our motivation is our desire to serve for self-gratification, studying is the goal and becomes more important than serving the teacher.

If the environment around us does not praise the glory of the Creator, as it should, we will never be able to attain a spiritual degree. Therefore, it is always recommended that we as students regard ourselves as the lowest (spiritually) compared to our group. This enables the student to adopt the state of mind of the collective. Our environment is necessary to attain the purpose of creation, which is why you should "buy yourself a friend."

Efforts in circulating Kabbalah help to accelerate the changes more than anything. Things will change anyway; the only question is how long the process will take—a day, a month, our entire life? The next degree is right around the corner, and it is in our power to soar to it right now! It depends on us alone and no one else!

When we study to attain the Spiritual World, time is of crucial importance, as we must first grow accustomed to spiritual concepts and definitions, and then live in them. By "time," we mean that changes occur in us consistently and at a great speed. We don't feel them; in fact, we may feel as though nothing is happening. Only afterwards do we suddenly and very profoundly realize all the changes that have occurred.

This is a result of those little inner changes that we do not feel. Our sensitivity threshold is very high and only from a certain degree onward do we begin to feel those changes. Everything that goes through us leaves its mark on our souls, and after some time the change suddenly appears. Therefore, the most important thing to do is to read, all the time, no matter how much of the text we absorb.

There are texts that must be read and reread according to the general curriculum, and there are texts that one should read only when in the mood. Such are letters or articles about the feeling of the spiritual. It is said that when we ascend, when we feel close to the material, it is good to read just the things that touch our feelings; i.e., where understanding will come through our hearts. The problem in attaining the spiritual is that we do not have the correct senses to do so. The spiritual can be acquired slowly and gradually when the heart allows it. Thus, there is a time to use the brain, and there is a time to use the heart.

Sometimes when we simply hold a book of Kabbalah, we immediately get all sorts of disturbances that "crawl" into our minds, until we just want to drop our studies. But as soon as we are sent pain from Above, we should take a Kabbalah book in our hand and then we will have no problem focusing on its words.

All that the Creator created is a desire to enjoy. In humans, that desire is developed more than in all other animals. The goal of the Creator is for humankind to be like Him: complete and eternal. But that goal can be attained only through the influence of pleasure or pain. Because we are made to enjoy and to feel pleasure, we cannot *not* feel anything. We feel the scarcity of pleasure as agony. When pleasure comes, we accept it as natural and take it for granted, thinking, "I deserve it." When pain comes, we resent it and feel, "I don't deserve this." Again, this stems from the fact that we are born of a substance called "desire to enjoy."

Because the Creator has a desire to bestow upon His creatures, He created us with a desire to enjoy. But if we were influenced by pleasure alone, because we are made solely from a desire to enjoy, we would turn into such egoists that we would become stupid. Thus, only the search for pleasure forces us to develop. In order to bring us to the complete development, meaning to be like the Creator, there is only one option: bestowal.

When we receive pleasure, we think we deserve it, but as soon as we feel pain, we begin to search for its source. Thus, we gradually come to the Creator, the origin of both pleasure and pain. Pain creates in us a desire to find its source, to know the Creator. Otherwise, we would never know the Creator and would never be able to equalize with Him.

If we are told that studying Kabbalah is good for us, how can we strengthen ourselves along the way? The Creator sends us disturbances so that we will learn by overcoming them how to approach Him. And if the disturbances cannot bring us enough strength to overcome them, we are sent more agony to force us to make an extra effort to overcome them. At that point, the disturbances no longer frighten us because the fear of pain forces us to be on constant alert. And this is the way! You, after all, want to attain the greatest thing there is, not just in our world, but anywhere!

As we study, many questions arise. It is important to understand that a question is a Vessel, and what matters is the Vessel. Once it is completed, the Light (the answer) immediately fills it. If we're ready for the answer, we feel the Upper Light to the extent of the ripeness of our will. If we're not ready for the answer, we do not feel the Light.

The Upper Light is at eternal rest. It is always in us. Despite the fact that the Light and the Vessel have opposite attributes, when the Light fills the Vessel, they become whole, one. Answers come precisely where there are questions.

The Creator and the creature merge into one attribute, although the creature doesn't feel it. Kabbalists don't hide this merging; on the contrary, they emphasize it. They do it so that others will realize that their efforts are meant to help them discover for themselves what is always within, but is concealed because of our current corrupted state.

CHAPTER 8.
EIGHT BEGINNING LESSONS IN KABBALAH

INTRODUCTION

Prior to experiencing the spiritual worlds for ourselves, everything we know about them comes to us from the writings of people who accomplished this same task before us. In those writings, they tell us about the entire structure of the spiritual worlds in great detail. These wonderful people that provide us with such a magnificent gift are called Kabbalists. Luckily, their writings also include how we can establish that same kind of contact, enter places that we currently do not perceive, and then experience the exact same things they did.

It turns out that these writings can be looked at in two ways: first, as a blueprint of what is in the spiritual and second, as an instruction manual that allows us to personally confirm everything they tell us. The end result of this wonderful legacy Kabbalists have so generously provided is that we are able to gain the exact same knowledge and actually perceive the exact same perfection they did. By following this "spiritual highway" they have provided us, we can gain a complete understanding of the goal of creation and are able to grasp its purpose, all while living in this world.

The following eight lessons are based upon a course given by Dr. Michael Laitman, my teacher and a Kabbalist. He designed his course based designed based upon three sources: Rabbi Shimon Bar Yochai's Zohar written in the 2nd century CE; the works of the Ari, Rav Y. Luria, and a Kabbalist who lived in Safed in the 16th century; and finally, the works of Rav Yehuda Ashlag, known as Baal HaSulam, and lived in the middle of the 20th century.

Actually, these three sources wrote about exactly the same thing, but in totally different eras, and using language that fit the students of their respective era. For more information on these sources, flip back to Chapter 5, Research Materials of Kabbalah.

Most of the material studied in Kabbalah is written in Hebrew, a language Abraham developed for the sole purpose of describing the spiritual. Although much of the following information in the lessons is put in a format that requires no true understanding of Hebrew, some of the more important Hebrew terms have been retained as they are and you are provided with an accurate definition for each term. You will notice that they are all *italicized* and the first letter is always Capitalized. Original diagrams with English labels have also been inserted to help you grasp the original diagrams with English labels to help you grasp the concepts with clarity and in a more simplified manner than would be required if only the Hebrew terms were given. Some of the diagrams might seem backwards to readers of English because Hebrew is read right-to-left.

These lessons are an explanation of one single thing, the process of creation. This is exactly what Kabbalah describes, and nothing else. The reason is simple. If we know where we came from, if we have a blueprint to use, we can follow this same blueprint right back up, step by step, to a total and complete revelation of the Creator.

The name given to Yehuda Ashlag, Baal HaSulam, means "Owner of the Ladder," because of the *Sulam* (Ladder) commentary on *The Zohar*. In other words, the texts we study certainly provide anyone who is only seeking knowledge with the information needed to answer questions about where we come from. But this is not their purpose. The great works we study are not for knowledge, but rather to provide us with the experience of these worlds for ourselves.

You will also notice that the word "phase" is used. You should think of it as a different part of the process, just as we go through different phases of development in our growth from childhood to adulthood. There are many phases in that process, and we most certainly change, but we remain "us".

It is very important to realize that this material is simply an overview. It is not a full, complete, and detailed explanation of Creation. In fact, it is not even a preface for that incredible process, but more of a preface to the preface. The true study of Kabbalah goes into incredible detail of the process of creation, providing the minutest of details.

For those of you who studied science in college, you can compare this chapter to eight quick lessons on Physics or Chemistry. While those eight lessons may provide you with an idea of the subject, there is no way one can explain such a vast subject as Creation in such few short pages.

Finally, this material should not be read quickly or scanned. Take your time. Allow yourself the luxury of absorbing what is written for more than simple knowledge. You may even want to go back and read these lessons multiple times in order go grasp what you may have missed. With that in mind, let's get started.

LESSON 1

In his writings, Rav Yehuda Ashlag explains to us that the Light emanating from the Creator designates the desire to create beings and to please them. You might remember that Light is the sensation of the Creator, pleasure. This in Kabbalah we refer to as the Root Phase and is numbered zero (0). In Hebrew, we call it Phase *Shoresh* and name it *Keter*. It is given the number 0 because it is considered the preliminary phase to actually creating anything at all. It is simply a desire to please and create something in which to give pleasure.

So at this point, all that we can say about Phase 0 (*Keter*) is that the Creator wishes to please, has a desire to bestow, to give, and begins the process of creating something that can receive what He wishes to give, namely pleasure. While continuing with the lesson, it may help you to refer to Figure 1.

In the second stage, referred to as Phase 1 in Hebrew - Phase *Aleph* (*Hochma*) — this Light creates a Vessel (in Hebrew - *Kli*). A *Kli* is something that has the ability to enclose a substance. It has boundaries. And just as the glass blower creates a glass to hold water or other beverages, this Vessel is created to hold something within it, that being pleasure.

The Vessel is created in such a way that it is perfectly suited to fulfill this purpose. In other words, the Vessel is the desire to receive pleasure in a perfect manner. To understand the relationship between the Light and the Vessel, one can think of a stamp and the imprint it makes.

An even simpler analogy might be if we imagine we are on a beach. If we press our hands into the wet sand and then lift our hands out, we will leave excellent imprints of our hands. If the sand is fine enough, we can even see the lines within the palm of the hand on the imprint.

The Bible tells us that God created man in His own image. That is exactly what I am referring to. The Vessel is designed in just this way, where the Vessel, this desire to receive pleasure, perfectly matches the Light that fills it completely and pleases it.

The Light itself has one single characteristic, one attribute, which is to please, to delight, to give pleasure. The attribute of the Vessel is the exact opposite. It is the perfect will to receive, the desire to experience

---

Figure 1. Five *Behinot*

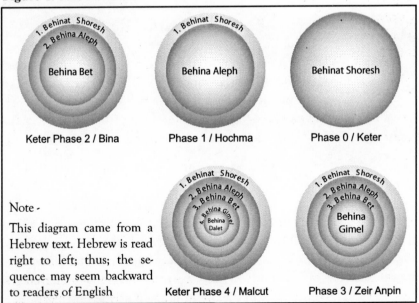

Note -

This diagram came from a Hebrew text. Hebrew is read right to left; thus; the sequence may seem backward to readers of English

83

pleasure. So the Light creates the Vessel, and then fills it completely. But when the Vessel is filled, it not only feels pleasure, but also feels what the Giver is like; it feels the Giver's attribute of bestowal. This exact experience of feeling who is giving that pleasure causes the next phase of creation to happen.

The experience of not only feeling pleasure but also feeling the property of the Giver, bestowal, can be thought of as transference. What is transferred to the Vessel is that very attribute of the Creator. This transference causes the Vessel to now wish to become like the Light. In other words, the Vessel feels this property of the Giver and wants to do what the Light can do, to give without restraint, to be like the Giver. But the Vessel has absolutely nothing to give. It is built for receiving. So in order to come as close as it can to giving, it stops receiving altogether. This stage we call Phase 2 - Phase *Bet* (*Bina*).

Now we have a serious predicament. The Vessel, which is now empty of Light because it felt the Creator and wishes to be like the Light, refuses to receive. The Light cannot perform what it is supposed to do and the Vessel cannot do what it is supposed to do. If the Vessel had anything to give, it would. But all it can do is the next best thing: refuse to receive any pleasure. This leads directly to the next stage which Kabbalah refers to as Phase 3 - *Gimel* (*Zeir Anpin*). The Vessel knows that the goal of the Light is to create and delight it. It also knows that its very existence is based on receiving pleasure, that it must receive a certain portion of the Light or it ceases to exist. In short, receiving is the Vessel's nature.

How can the Vessel accomplish fulfilling what it needs and at the same time fulfill its desire to be like its Creator? Phase 3, *Zeir Anpin* (ZA), provides the answer. It is in fact, a mixed phase and the only possible answer to this problem. The Vessel decides it will receive a portion of the Light, but with one rather incredible stipulation. It will only receive Light if it is doing so in order to delight the One who created it. Let's repeat that. The Vessel knows it must receive and will do so, but only if it can perform its function with the intent of pleasing the Giver.

What actually happens here is very important. The Vessel, the will to receive, now has two different attributes it can compare with each other. It knows what the desire of the Giver feels like, and it knows what its own nature is, receiving. It has the desire to be like its Creator - to bestow—and it has the desire to receive delight. But it also knows that its true nature is one of total and complete reception, something it cannot change. It realizes that it is far more natural for it to receive than to give, for this is exactly how it was created. What has happened here is a discovery. Before, this Vessel had not realized its own nature was the opposite of its Giver, and now it does. This leads to the 4th phase Kabbalah calls Phase *Dalet* (*Malchut*).

This realization of its own true nature leads the Vessel to a decision that it must do as it was designed and receive all the pleasure the Light brings, all one hundred percent of it. *Something special has happened here; an independent decision*. In the previous three phases, the Vessel was only reacting under the power of the Light. But in the fourth phase, the desire to receive one hundred percent of the Light once more, is a completely independent decision. This is what distinguishes this phase from Phase 1, Phase *Aleph* (*Hochma*). In both phases, the Vessel is only receiving but in this last phase, the Vessel now has its own independent desire. This independence is what allows us to call it a "creature" or "the Creation." In other words, the reception of pleasure was the Vessel's choice, not the Creator's.

It can now be called "the creature" because the desire actually came from within itself, not directly from the Light where the Light was simply filling it with no decision on the Vessel's part. What gave it this distinction is the choice. It can receive or not receive. What decision did it make? It chose to receive, accepting everything once more. Prior to this, it was filled only because it was what the Creator wanted. In other words, the very first independent desire to receive pleasure from the Light has now been born totally within the created being.

This concept is so fundamental to our work! Let's look at an example. Consider the process of birth. No matter what we do before we are born, we receive all of our nourishment whether we want it or not; every need is met by our mothers. We have absolutely no choice in the matter. All of our systems are completely dictated by what our mothers provided for us within the womb.

Yet once we make that long trip down the birth canal and announce our presence to the world, usually with a hair-raising scream, everything changes. The moment that umbilical cord is cut, our systems begin to act independently. We begin to breathe air on our own. Our blood supply is independent. Our nourishment must come from an external source and into our mouths. Certainly our parents may still force many things within our lives, but now, when we are hungry, we cry. When we need to be changed, we let Mom and Dad know it. The process of an independent creation has taken place.

Now let's discuss for a moment the way Kabbalah names Light. This will be easier if you will refer to the list below. We have five phases:

- Phase Zero – *Shoresh*, named *Keter*
- Phase One – *Aleph*, named *Hochma*
- Phase Two – *Bet*, named *Bina*
- Phase Three – *Gimel*, named *Zeir Anpin*
- Phase Four – *Dalet*, named *Malchut*

A quick check with an English-to-Hebrew Dictionary will confirm that *Aleph*, *Bet*, *Gimel*, and *Dalet* are the first four letters of the Hebrew alphabet. It is important to note that the names, *Keter*, *Hochma*, *Bina*, *Zeir Anpin*, and *Malchut* are not names of creatures, but rather names of phases in the process of creation. So when we say *Malchut*, we are talking about the creature as it is in that stage.

In each phase, there is a different kind of Light, at least from our perspective. In reality, there is never anything but one Light, and the difference we sense is completely and totally because of our own perception. The Root Phase, Phase Zero, *Shoresh*, corresponds to a Light called *Keter*. Phase one, *Hochma*, corresponds to a Light called *Hochma*. Phase 2, *Bina*, corresponds to a Light called *Hassadim*. Phase 3, *Zeir Anpin*, corresponds to a combination of the first two Lights, both *Hochma* and *Hassadim*. Phase 4, *Malchut*, corresponds to the Light of *Hochma* once again.

Phase	Behina / Sefira	Type of Light	World	Desire
Shoresh (root; zero)	Keter	Ohr Keter	Adam Kadmon	To bestow
Aleph (one)	Hochma	Ohr Hochma (Wisdom) Ohr Haya (Life)	Atzilut	Unconscious desire to receive
Bet (two)	Bina	Ohr Hassadim (Mercy)	Beria	Desire to give without receiving Light
Gimel (three)	Zeir Anpin (ZA) / Tifferet	Large (90%) Ohr Hassadim Small (10%) Ohr Hochma	Yetzira	Desire to receive while giving
Dalet (four)	Malchut / Olam Ein Sof (World of Infinity)	Ohr Hochma overtakes Ohr Hassadim	Assiya (Kingdom of desires)	Expressed desire to receive

LEVELS ABOVE CREATION

KLI

Table 1.

The Hebrew word for Light is *Ohr*. Those astute readers will see the correlation between *Ohr Hochma* and the Creator giving pleasure, as well as *Ohr Hassadim*, the creature rejecting pleasure.

Our entire existence is based upon one single fact. All that exists in this entire universe is the Creator's desire to delight us and our desire

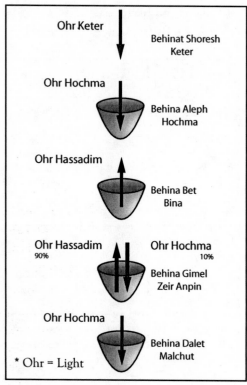

Figure 2.
Four Phases of Emanation of Light

for that pleasure. Everything in the universe happens the way it does because of this law. We are completely and totally under its rule. All different kinds of existence, be them inanimate, vegetative, animate, or speaking, every single solitary thing wants to receive pleasure, to receive a spark of the Light.

We were created with only one purpose, that when we receive the Light from the Creator, we feel infinite and everlasting pleasure, not in a selfish way, but rather in a perfect and an absolute way. If the Light enters the Vessel and fills it up completely, then this Vessel can no longer receive because the desire is saturated by the Light; and in the absence of a desire, the pleasure passes away as well. It is a vicious circle. We want pleasure, we receive pleasure, the pleasure kills the desire, and so the pleasure is no longer felt. It is this exact problem that the spiritual system of Kabbalah cures.

We can only receive endlessly when we do not receive for our own sake, i.e. we enjoy for the sake of the Giver. Then the Light entering the Vessel does not neutralize the desire to receive. Through experience we all know that when we are hungry and begin to eat, after a certain time we no longer feel the hunger, even if the most delicious dishes are made available. Pleasure is experienced on the borderline between pleasure itself and the desire for it. However, as soon as pleasure enters the desire and starts to satisfy it, this desire slowly fades away. And if the pleasure is stronger than the desire, this can even lead to repulsion.

So we have a problem here, but the good news is we have a solution as well. The Creator devised a system that gives His creature a remedy for its predicament. If we choose to feel pleasure while pleasing others instead of feeling it within ourselves, the pleasure never ends. You see, this pleasure relies on how much you can give. The more pleasure you give to people, the more pleasure you get to feel. In other words, I live outside myself, outside my own will to receive. This condition produces an eternal existence, the state of perfection, which is one of the attributes of the Creator. This is exactly the state the Creator wants to usher us into.

At first glance, this idea seems totally preposterous. But think about it for a moment. Suppose everything as we know it was actually backward, and instead of experiencing pleasure when someone does something for you, it was the other way around. Imagine that every time you did something for someone else, you received this incredible pleasure far surpassing any pleasure you ever received by doing something for yourself or receiving from another.

In that case, we would be lining up to give, and to whom would not make a bit of difference. The more we gave, the more pleasure we would receive. In the blink of an eye, our entire world would change. And as crazy as it sounds, this is exactly the destination to which we are heading.

If the creature, the Vessel, chooses only to receive, it finds itself caught in a trap. The problem is that in receiving for itself, it only feels whatever is inside of it. If the creature could feel the Creator's pleasure from delighting the creation, it would endlessly experience the pleasure, just like a mother, who selflessly gives to her children. But in its current state, everybody loses.

Fortunately, we have an absolutely perfect system in which to exist, and just as unfortunately, we choose not to exist in it. Right at our fingertips, we have unlimited knowledge, infinite existence, a feeling of eternity and harmony. Within this system, the Creator constantly pours Light on to its creature. But the creature only receives the Light if by doing so it delights the Creator. Kabbalah refers to this system as Returning Light (*Ohr Hozer*), as opposed to the Direct Light (*Ohr Yashar*) the Creator sends. See Figure-3.

But for this system to exist, the creature must first have a desire that attracts that Direct Light toward it. Previously we have spoken about a screen that reflects, just like an ear drum or the retina of the eye. This is where that screen enters the picture. A screen must be placed between that Direct Light and the creature.

This screen, known in Kabbalah as a *Masach* (pronounced ma-ssah), prevents the creature from receiving for its own sake. It only allows the creature to accept an amount of Light in proportion to its own strength; to accept it only for the sake of the Creator. Kabbalah calls this action "receiving in order to bestow." In this way, the creature can resemble the Creator, be like Him. In other words, the following exchange takes place: the Creator sends pleasure to the creature, who accepts it under the exclusive condition that by doing so it pleases the Creator.

Baal HaSulam quotes the very simple and eternal example of the guest and the host. The host presents to his guest a table full of delicacies. The guest sits down but dares not eat because he does not want to be in a position to receive and he is not certain if the host is sincere in his desire to delight him. The guest is embarrassed because he has nothing to offer in return and can only receive while the host gives. That is why the guest refuses what is offered in order to understand the host's true desire.

If the host insists, asking his guest to honor the food and assuring him that he will be very pleased if he does so, then the guest will start eating. He will do so because he is convinced that this will please the host and he no longer feels that he is receiving from the host, but is giving to him, i.e., he gives his host pleasure.

The roles have been reversed. Even if it is the host who has prepared all the food and acts as the inviter, he clearly understands that the fulfillment of his desire to please depends uniquely on his guest. The guest holds the key to the success of the dinner and consequently masters the situation.

The Creator has especially made the creature in such a way that under the influence of the Light it will feel ashamed of only receiving. The creature, using its freedom of choice freely, will finally reach a level where it does not experience pleasure selfishly, but to please the Creator. These divine attributes, these feelings, are beyond description and we cannot understand them. The entrance into the spiritual worlds by acquiring just one degree of similitude with the Creator already means eternity, absolute pleasure, and attainment.

The science of Kabbalah studies the unfolding of creation. It describes the path along which our world and all other worlds —indeed the whole universe—must tread while achieving its progressive correction (*Tikkun*) to reach the level of the Creator, the ultimate degree of perfection and eternity. We need to undertake this work of correction while living in this world, in our everyday circumstances and dressed in our bodies.

Kabbalists have already reached this degree of perfection and described it for us. All souls without exception must reach this ultimate level in due time. Each one of us has to start from the beginning point and eventually reach the final point. There is no free will for this. Nor is there free will for us to alter the path, because everyone has to go through all the phases and feelings and progressively integrate them. In other words, we must "live" the path.

Let's return to the phases of creation. The phases of development of the creature are divided by what Kabbalah calls *Aviut* (pronounced Ah-vee-yut). The thickness or coarseness of the desire for delight is called

Aviut. What is thickness or coarseness? The farther away the creature is from the Creator, the more desire it feels, and the more Aviut it has. For instance, in the 0 Phase, Keter, and in Phase 1, Hochma, there is no (or hardly any) desire at all. There is almost no coarseness, no Aviut. Everything is under the power of the Creator, like an unborn baby that has everything done for it. But in the last phase, which is farthest from the Creator, Malchut, the creature, has the greatest intensity of desire to receive. It is good to remember that this desire to receive comes from its own decision, hence it is a selfish one, turned toward itself.

So the creature is now in that Phase 4, Malchut. As in the Phase 1, Hochma, the creature is simply receiving, and receiving 100%. You will also remember that during the stage of Hochma, the creature also was able to feel the attributes of the Creator. That is exactly what happens again. Malchut begins to feel the Giver. But this feeling of who is giving it pleasure is different than the first time. There is a huge difference in Phase 1-Hochma and Phase 4-Malchut. Malchut is an independent creature, making its own decision to receive, whereas in Hochma, the Creator controlled everything.

From the combination of feeling the Creator and having made its own decision to receive, an entirely new sensation is felt for the very first time, the sensation of shame. Malchut feels that its attribute of receiving is completely opposite of the Light and it has become aware of its own selfishness. Now this is no ordinary shame, as in what we feel when we are caught doing something bad, but immense and intense shame. This shame is felt so strongly that Malchut decides to stop receiving the Light, and that is exactly what it does.

This rejection of the Light by Malchut is called First Restriction. Restriction in Hebrew is Tzimtzum. Hebrew letters are also numbers; thus 1 is Aleph, or "first." And so Kabbalah calls this act Tzimtzum Aleph. Now once again, everything is in balance, but backward, as Malchut does not receive and the Creator does not give.

At this point, you are probably thinking, "Here we go again!" But rest assure that help is on the way. Now if we try to picture this in our mind, it may appear like some sort of massive pacing, drooling monster of desire, wanting and wanting and wanting, but it cannot take what it wants because of the torture it brings the poor miserable beast when it receives.

Our creature ponders endlessly, finally coming up with a solution. It will imitate our example of the guest and the host. *Malchut* can push away all the incoming Light because it does not want to feel like a receiver. Then it sets the condition that it will accept a portion of the Light, though not for its own delight, but because it wants to please the Creator, as it knows that the Creator wishes it delight.

Receiving in such a way is like giving, so *Malchut* is now in a position to be the giver. Remember, *Malchut* first rejects everything, then calculates how much it can receive for the Creator. Only after that calculation is made does *Malchut* take in even the most minuscule amount of Light, and of course, only with the intent to please the Creator.

What does all of the above tell us? What we have been describing is the birth of desire. If a true desire is to be brought to life, we see that the Light needs to undergo four different phases. We do not count the Root Phase. This is exactly what happens with every single desire you experience. Before those desires are felt inside us, that exact process occurs as it goes through all the phases of development of Light coming from the Creator until at last, we feel it. It is totally impossible for a desire to appear without the Light first. This is important: Light comes first, then the desire.

Now let's take a look at the structure of the creature, just as it is in *Malchut*, Phase 4. The creature is the Vessel. In the diagram below, there are several kinds of Light. The Direct Light, Light that shines directly from the Creator is called *Ohr Yashar*. The Light that the creature, *Malchut*, initially rejects is called *Ohr Hozer*. It is also known as Returning Light, which the screen does not allow within.

Finally, the Light that *Malchut* determines it can let inside, because the strength of its screen is strong enough that it can accept it for the sake of the Creator is called Inner Light, or *Ohr Pnimi* (pronounced

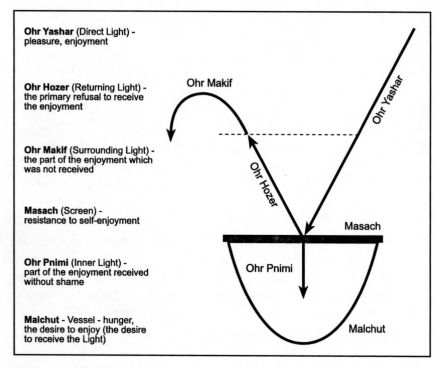

Ohr Yashar (Direct Light) -
pleasure, enjoyment

Ohr Hozer (Returning Light) -
the primary refusal to receive
the enjoyment

Ohr Makif (Surrounding Light) -
the part of the enjoyment which
was not received

Masach (Screen) -
resistance to self-enjoyment

Ohr Pnimi (Inner Light) -
part of the enjoyment received
without shame

Malchut - Vessel - hunger,
the desire to enjoy (the desire
to receive the Light)

Figure 3. The Vessel

Pnee-mee). We will get to the Surrounding Light Kabbalah calls *Ohr Makif* a bit later. Study this diagram until you are familiar with the terms and what they mean.

Remember our story about the guest and the host? When the guest faces the host and the table full of delicacies he first refuses everything, then decides to eat a bit in order to please the host even though he would like to gulp everything down in one go. This means that one must use his selfish desires, but in an altruistic way. As the guest starts to consider things, he understands that he cannot accept the whole dinner for the sake of the host; he only may accept a small portion of it.

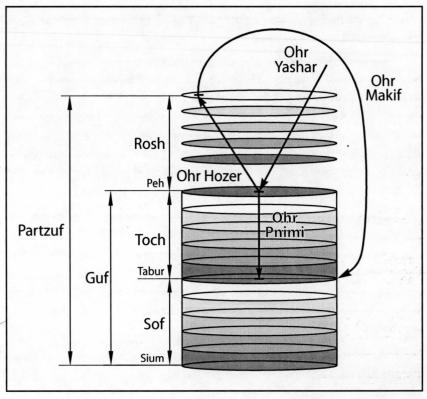

Figure 4. The *Partzuf*

Our creature applies this exact concept after making *Tzimtzum Aleph*, First Restriction. Remember that due to the intense shame *Malchut* felt after deciding to receive 100% of the Light, it performed *Tzimtzum Aleph* and took in nothing. But if it applies the above idea, it accepts just a small portion of the Light, let's say twenty percent, and then it pushes away the remaining eighty percent.

Now let's take a look at the creature that exists at the point where it decides to only take in an amount of Light that it can receive for the sake of the Creator. We call the combination of a Vessel and Light, a *Partzuf*, an emanated being, a creature that has made that decision to restrict everything it cannot take in with the intent to please the Creator. As with the previous names, *Partzuf* is the name of a condition of the creature, but a very important condition.

Kabbalah divides the *Partzuf* into three general areas: the Rosh, the *Toch*, and the *Sof*. The part of the created being that makes a decision on how much Light it may accept inside for the sake of the Creator is called Rosh (Head). Think of it as the calculating part, the part that looks at the data and determines what can be taken in based upon that data. The part accepting the Light is called *Toch* (inner part). The last part, which remains empty, is called *Sof* (End). This is the place where the created being performs a restriction and no longer accepts the Light.

You might also notice that within each general part, there are subparts that correspond to the overall five phases of creation, *Keter, Hochma, Bina, Zeir Anpin*, and *Malchut*. Each part of the *Partzuf* has a bit of the entire picture in it. This fact will be very important later on, but for now, it is good to remember that every single thing has those parts in it. No matter how we break down any part, it always contains those inner parts, and so on and so on into infinity!

As for how Kabbalah names things, different terms are assigned [or given] to the various parts of creation using names of various parts of the human body. There are no terms, labels or numbers in the spiritual worlds. It is nevertheless easier and more understandable to use words.

Kabbalists have chosen to express themselves in a very simple language because everything in our world results from the spiritual worlds, in accordance with the direct connections descending from Above downward. These connections run from every spiritual object to every object in our world. For everything that has a name in our world, we may take the name of an object of our world and use it to designate the spiritual object that begets it.

None of the authentic Kabbalah scripts mention our world, not in a single word, although they may be using the language of our world. Every object of our world refers to a matching object in the spiritual worlds, but Kabbalah speaks only about the spiritual. So when we speak about the part of the *Partzuf* that is responsible for thinking, the calculating and the analysis of data, it is called Head, or *Rosh*.

The screen, the *Masach*, lies between the *Rosh* and the *Toch* at a place called the Mouth or *Peh*. That part where the Light can enter is called the Body, or *Guf*. There is a part where the Light is not allowed to go because the creature has determined to only take in a certain amount. That part is called the *Sof*. The part that divides the *Toch* and *Sof* in the *Guf* is called the *Tabur*, or Navel in English. The lowest part of the *Partzuf* where absolutely no Light can be is called the *Sium*, meaning conclusion. The entire creature is called *Malchut*.

Let's take the example of a stone in our world. There is a Force Above that generates this stone: it will therefore be named "stone." The only difference is that the spiritual stone is a spiritual root endowed with specific attributes, which in turn matches a branch in our world, labeled "stone," a material object. This is how the language of branches was created. By means of names, denominations and actions in our world, we can refer back to elements and actions in the spiritual worlds. Thus, as it is above, so it is below.

LESSON 2

Congratulations! You have made it through the first lesson. But the question arises, "What does all of that have to do with me?" The answer is simple: "Literally everything." You see, we were created for only one reason: to receive complete, unlimited and absolute pleasure, delight. But in order to accomplish this, we must know how this system known as "the spiritual worlds" operates. Every law under which our corporeal world operates stems from the spiritual worlds. This is where our souls were before we were born, and this is where they return after our lives end.

However, we are only interested in the middle part, between those two events, that period where we are enclosed within this physical body and we have a heartbeat. This is precisely what Kabbalah helps us with—how to use everything in this life to accomplish the goal of experiencing the Creator. To ascend spiritually, we need to know everything and use all the possibilities we are offered.

First of all, we must know about what is all around us in this world in which we live. We need to understand the different categories of existence here: inanimate, vegetative, animate, and speaking, and how they work. Then, we must understand ourselves. I do not speak of the animal in which we are incased, but the soul within that animal. We need to understand how it grows, what part we can play in the soul's development, and then do all we can to advance in our spiritual ascent.

This does happen naturally, but the process is extremely slow, bloody, painful, and ends right where you are today – learning how to accelerate the process in a conscious manner. So we end up with a choice. We can either take the responsibility into our own hands and do what the Creator is moving us toward willingly, or we can be coerced into the process by the Creator through suffering. This latter path is called "the path of pain." As for myself, being a chicken at heart, I prefer the less painful path and will agree to do tons of work in order to avoid it.

The Wisdom of Kabbalah is not about how to take care of our problems in this world. It does not cure our financial difficulties or help us find a life mate. But it does tell us exactly how to meet our spiritual responsibilities, and not be forced to advance through more troubles. In that way, it helps us to solve the overall problem from which all of our daily problems are sent to us. All of our headaches and sufferings are thrown in front of us for a single reason: to bring us to the point of beginning our spiritual ascent.

But after we discover how everything works—the laws of the spiritual worlds, who sends them to us and why—we can use our everyday challenges to help us to behave correctly and move farther along toward the Creator.

Between the lowest part of the last spiritual world, the world of *Assiya*, and our world, this corporeal world in which we physically exist, lies a barrier known in Kabbalah as *Machsom*. Once we cross this barrier and enter the spiritual worlds, we begin a path of 6,000 steps toward the end result known as the End of Correction – *Gmar Tikkun*. Every single time we take another step up that ladder, it represents the removal of a layer of concealment of the Creator.

The End of Correction follows the correction of all our desires. The first stage in studying Kabbalah consists in reading as many pertinent books as possible and "digesting" as much knowledge as possible. The next stage is group work, when the student's and group's desires merge. The student's Vessel enlarges proportionately to the number of group members.

In the group work stage, it is the group that symbolizes the Creator, since everything located outside us is the Creator. Throughout time, Kabbalists have had groups. Only within the framework of a group and based on the mutual ties fostered by its members can students advance in their understanding of the spiritual worlds.

The study of Kabbalah is, in fact, a two-part process. In the first part, we study creation and its ascent from that initial thought of the Creator right down to the level of Our World. The second part is the study of the trip back up, from where we exist today all the way back up the same path to the highest level. It is important to note that the physical body does not go anywhere; we remain right where we are. We ascend in a spiritual way that arises from our efforts and the development resulting from those efforts.

In our first lesson, we learned about the initial stages of the process of creation and the parts of the creature. Now that we have learned a bit about the creature's anatomy, let's continue. You will remember that the creature decided not to take in all the light, but only a part of it, say 20%. The other 80% was left outside. That Light is called Surrounding Light, or *Ohr Makif*.

The Light that is taken within is located in the *Toch*, the body, and the Surrounding Light, the *Ohr Makif* begins to influence the creature now. It says, "You see how pleasant it is to accept a portion of the Light? You do not know how much pleasure remains outside, just try to accept some more." We can understand that it is better not to experience pleasure at all than to experience just a tiny bit of it. Pleasure exerts pressure both from outside and inside and it therefore becomes much more difficult to oppose. Ever try to eat just one potato chip?

In many ways, it is much easier not to eat any potato chips at all if we can only eat one. We can go for days, weeks, or months without a chip, but can we eat just one? The *Partzuf* is the same way. As long is it was not taking in any Light at all, it could remain in that state for a long time. But now that Light is inside, it is like enjoying the taste of the potato chip as you eat it, and also looking down seeing the whole bag lying there. There is pressure from two places, not one. You are enjoying it on the inside, and see there is plenty more as well.

The *Partzuf* is being pressured from both inside and outside now. But it has already calculated how much it can take in for the sake of the Creator. If it takes in even the smallest amount of extra Light, that tiny bit of Light dooms it to receiving for itself and feeling that horrid shame, which is much worse than not getting the pleasure.

There is only one thing it can do. It can only reject the Light it has within in order so it can return to its initial state of emptiness before accepting any Light inside. And this is exactly what our creature, the *Partzuf*, does. The Light taken within for the sake of the Creator is called *Ohr Pnimi*. The Surrounding Light that was the Light not allowed within is called *Ohr Makif*.

The pressure these two Lights exert at the same time on the screen (*Masach*) in the navel (*Tabur*), which is that border in the *Partzuf* that separates the *Toch* and the *Sof*, is called the "beating within and without." In Hebrew it is called *Bitush Pnimi uMakif*. In other words, these two Lights exerted pressure on the border that divides the areas where the creature accepted pleasure and did not accept pleasure.

What is actually occurring inside the *Partzuf?* The Light was taken inside the mouth, the *Peh*, and shoved the screen down to the level of the *Tabur* that equaled that 20% the creature calculated it could accept for the sake of the Creator. The *Tabur* (the Navel) is the place in the *Guf* (the body), where the creature decides it must not take any Light lower into the *Guf*. When the creature determines it cannot handle the pressure and must expel the Light from its body, the *Masach* (screen) rises back up to the mouth (*Peh*), shoving the Light away. Actually it is not that the creature cannot handle the pressure. It turns out that what the creature discovers is that this is not satisfying the goal, to receive only in order to please the Creator.

So how did the creature know how much to take in? How did it arrive at that figure of 20%? That is the *Rosh's* department. Before the creature ever let any Light within the *Toch*, it had every bit of information it needed to make the decision. It knew what kind of Light it was, what kind of delight it would bring, what its own desire was, and how strong its force is opposed to the delight for its own sake.

Remember that the first thing the *Partzuf* does is to <u>refuse</u> the Light, rejecting it completely. That Light is called *Ohr Hozer* (Returning Light). Within that Light is all of the information that is needed for the *Rosh* to calculate. According to this information, as well as the information remaining from the state when the *Partzuf* was filled with Light, and from the state following the restriction of the Light, the *Partzuf* keeps a memory of the past, an imprint called *Reshimo*.

So what really exists in the spiritual? Only the desire to delight and the delights that satisfy that desire. You might remember the term, *Aviut*, all the information about the desire the creature has. The *Rosh* has this as well as information about the Light. The process of expansion of that Light within the *Partzuf* is called *Hitlabshut* (clothing). One can truly say that there is only the Creator and Creation.

Every time the creature expels the Light and then begins calculating, it has information from its previous state. It has a memory of the desire

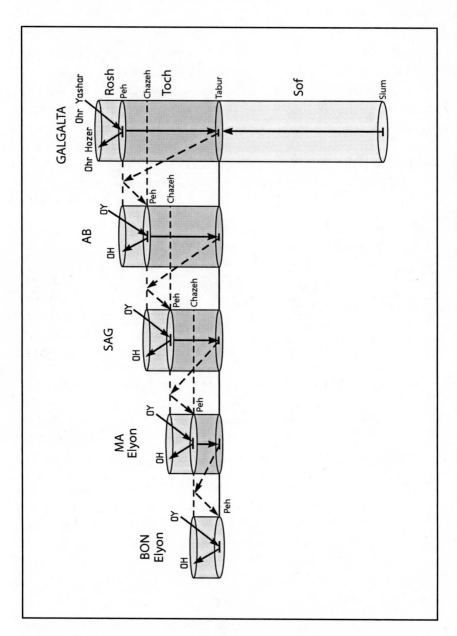

Figure 5. Five *Partzufim*: *Galgalta*, AB, SAG, MA, BON

and a memory what the Light was like. In Kabbalistic terms, it has *Reshimo* of *Aviut* (the desire) and *Hitlabshut* (the Light). That is all it needs in order to know precisely what it felt when the Light was last taken in. Now it can make proper calculations about what to do next and how to carry it out.

The first time the Light is taken within the *Partzuf* is called *Galgalta*. After the creature rejects the Light because the pressure is too great for it to handle, it attempts to once again take in the Light, say 15%. But in order to do that, the *Toch* must shrink, and that is exactly what it does. The *Toch* (Interior) decreases in size, allowing the *Rosh* (Head) to only reach where the *Peh* (Mouth) once was. The new place of the *Peh* is in a place called *Chazeh* (Chest) of the prior *Partzuf*, *Galgalta*. This new *Partzuf* is called AB. We will have more on this process later.

There are actually five different *Partzufim* (plural for *Partzuf*) in a spiritual world. Their names are *Galgalta*, AB, SAG, MA, and BON. Remember, a *Partzuf* is a spiritual phase, a mechanism of calculations that is independently calculating how to correct itself where it can receive in order to bestow to the Creator. In each *Partzuf*, less and less Light is taken within.

So how are the levels of *Aviut* (desire) and *Hitlabshut* (Light) determined? Actually this begins back at the start where *Galgalta* is determined to have an *Aviut* of level 4 and a desire of level 4. Remember that it took in all the Light, then rejected it. It had the maximum levels of both Light and desire. We shorten the way this is written to (Light, Desire), and in this case (4,4) when talking about these determining factors for making calculations.

The next *Partzuf*, in this new case called AB, keeps that data and lowers its level to match a (4,3) level – Light level 4 and desire level of only 3. That way it knows it can take in the Light safely.

For SAG, the level will be (3,2) and so on. Each *Partzuf* lowers its capacity to fill its body, the *Guf*, with Light for the sake of the Creator more and more. It is also important to note that nothing is ever lost in spirituality. Each preceding part is within the current part. So in reality, what is really being described here is a system, not an evolution.

As previously stated, there are five *Partzufim* to each world and there are five worlds: *Olam Adam Kadmon* (*Olam* means world), *Olam Atzilut, Olam Beria, Olam Yetzira,* and finally *Olam Assiya.* Five worlds with five *Partzufim* each means that altogether there are twenty-five *Partzufim,* which emerge from above to below. There will be much more about them later on.

Our world is a state of *Malchut* (absolute will to receive) that is characterized by the absence of a screen, meaning it lacks the basic requirement to be considered a *Partzuf.*

Flip back to the diagram (Figure 4) in the previous lesson and take a quick look again. In the *Partzuf* shown, there are actually two different conditions it can be in. The first condition is when it accepts Light from the Creator and enjoys the pleasure. This condition is called *Hochma.* Remember the first phase, Phase *Aleph* called *Hochma* when the Creator's Light entered the Vessel and pleased it? One might wonder if there is any correlation between that phase and this condition. Rest assure that it is not coincidental.

The second condition is when the *Partzuf* only wants to give and be like the Creator, and also enjoys that state. This condition is called *Bina.* Remember that the second phase, known as Phase *Bet,* is called *Bina* as well. It is rather obvious that these two conditions, *Hochma* and *Bina,* are exact opposites. The first has to do with receiving and the second has to do with giving.

Actually, there is a third condition as well. It is a mixed one where the creature takes in some of the Light, but only the amount it can receive in order to please the Creator. The rest of the *Partzuf* remains empty. By now you have probably guessed that this condition is called *Zeir Anpin.*

It is important to know that there are two kinds of Light. Light of *Hochma* is the Light of pleasure. Light of *Hassadim* is the Light of correction. It is the Light that builds the *Masach,* the screen we have been talking about. So as an example, let's say we have ten percent of the Light of *Hochma* and ninety percent of the Light of *Hassadim*. This condition would fall under the category of "mixed" and be called *Zeir Anpin*.

The absolute final stage is our beastly creature, *Malchut*. It is the genuine 100% no-holds-barred, "give-it-to-me-because-I-want-it" stage of desire to receive. This condition has another name, *Ein Sof*, which means "World of Infinity." Infinity here is not like the scientific term, infinity, but rather relates to unlimited receiving, the characteristic of *Malchut*. This is what happened right before the first restriction; *Malchut* devoured everything by its own choice. But it also suffered the consequences, the incredible feeling of shame.

Actually, this initial acceptance of every bit of the Light is an absolute necessity. In order to feel the spiritual shame resulting from receiving without giving in return, it is first necessary to perceive the Creator, to perceive His properties, to feel Him as the Giver, to see His glory. Then the comparison between His properties and the creature's own egoistic nature will bring about the feeling of shame.

We are no different. Our first task is to simply perceive the Creator. But this requires a lot of work all in itself. The glory of the spiritual, the Creator, does not just happen all at once; it unfolds in front of us. As it does, the first thing that appears in us is a desire to do something for Him.

We see this all the time in our world. When someone has the opportunity to do something for a very famous person, such as a movie star or a government leader, they will do it with pleasure and enjoyment. If the President of the U.S. or our favorite movie star asked a personal favor from any of us, no matter what our political affiliation, we would probably jump to do it simply because of the great importance of the person requesting it. This type of work is considered a privilege, not work, because we receive so much pleasure from "being allowed" to do the task.

The aim of our entire work is the revelation of the Creator, His Glory, and His Might. Once this level is reached, what we witness will serve us as the source of energy to do something for the Creator's benefit. This revelation of the Creator, it should be emphasized, will occur only when a person has already acquired a definite desire to use the revelation only for altruistic purposes, i.e., to attain the altruistic attributes, or bestowal.

Now back to our creature. *Malchut* rejected all 100% of that Light and is actually still willing to receive Light, but does not want to use its own will to gobble everything it can. It knows that if it acts with its own will and receives for its own sake, it moves farther from the Creator. It then makes the First Restriction, called *Tzimtzum Aleph*. By doing this it returns to the state of emptiness, but it also likens itself to the Creator.

This act of giving away causes a feeling of being absolute and complete. It may seem that being empty and complete contradict each other. But I am not talking about empty as in hungry. This emptiness is a lack of need of pleasure. In our world, this would correspond to being satisfied. This is because the delight received does not disappear. The one who is doing the giving feels the one who is receiving constantly while giving to him and sending him pleasure. So the creature is able to constantly feel the delight and in two ways, in quality and in quantity.

The Creator created Vessels in an absolutely ingenious way. They are organized in such a way that they progressively absorbed the Light's attribute of giving relentlessly. Through the process of this absorption, they became similar to the Light. But how in the world can *Malchut* be similar to the Light and still receive delight?

Earlier, we talked about how *Malchut* placed a *Masach*, a screen, on all of its desires, making it impossible to receive for its own sake. So when the Light comes to *Malchut*, the creature pushes away every bit of the pleasure. Next it decides that it will only take in as much Light as it can to please the Creator. If it does receive in this manner, it is the same as giving without restraint.

From the condition of *Malchut* in the World of *Ein Sof* where *Malchut* was still gobbling up everything it could, then made the *Tzimtzum Aleph*, there remains a memory, a *Reshimo*. This *Reshimo* is composed of: (i) level 4 *Hitlabshut* (information about the quality and quantity of Light) and (ii) level 4 *Aviut* (information about the force of desire). Using these two kinds of memory, *Reshimo* of the Light and the desire, *Malchut* carries out a calculation in its *Rosh* (head). It determines that it is able to receive the first twenty percent of Light for the sake of the Creator.

Let's break this down in percentages, observe what is happening, and see where all this Light is going. 100% of the Light that comes to *Malchut* is called *Ohr Yashar* (Direct Light). That entire amount of Light is rejected and is called *Ohr Hozer* (Returning Light). *Malchut* decides to take in 20% of the Light. That twenty percent of the Light that enters inside is called *Ohr Pnimi* (Inner Light). The greatest part of the Light, the remaining 80% left outside, is called *Ohr Makif* (Surrounding Light).

You will remember that there are five *Partzufim* in each world in the spiritual. The *Partzufim* are called *Galgalta*, AB, SAG, MA, and BON. *Galgalta* was the first *Partzuf* to receive a portion of the Light. After the creature decided the pressure from both within and without to accept more Light was too great, it expelled the entire amount of the Light. This was because even if it took in the smallest amount of additional Light, it would feel immense shame.

As the Light enters the *Partzuf*, the screen lowers from the *Peh* to the *Tabur*. As *Galgalta* pushes away the Light, the screen returns to the *Peh* (Mouth) that divides the *Rosh* (Head) and *Toch* (Interior) and once again the *Partzuf* is empty. At this point all is fine once more because no pleasure can be felt in this state. As the screen rises back to the *Peh*, it weakens and the *Aviut* decreases.

This entire process of withdrawal of the Light in a *Partzuf* is known as Refinement, *Hizdakchut* in Hebrew. But on the other hand, during the *Hitpashtut* (expansion of the Light into the *Partzuf*), the screen becomes coarser. In other words, the *Aviut* actually increases.

This increasing and decreasing *Aviut* (desire) makes sense if we actually look at what is happening. As the Light enters the *Partzuf* and lowers the screen, more and more pressure is placed on the screen that keeps out the Light. This is because the screen is being pressured by the *Ohr Pnimi*, the Light inside it, and also by the *Ohr Makif*, the Light outside it. As the pressure increases, so does the desire. But as the screen rises and pushes out the Light, the pressure weakens. As the pressure from the outside and inside weakens, the desire (*Aviut*) lowers.

Once all of the Light was rejected from *Galgalta*, the creature still had memories. Those *Reshimot* (plural for *Reshimo*) were all about the quality of the Light, as well as how much was taken in, (level 4 *Hitlabshut*), and *Reshimot* about the force of the desire *Galgalta* had (*Aviut*).

But the level of desire that registered was not level 4, it was level 3. Why? One measure of *Aviut* disappeared because the *Partzuf* realized that it is impossible for it to work with a desire in that fourth level. So now the *Reshimot* are written as (4,3), Light of level 4, but force of desire on level 3.

So because the *Aviut* lowered to level 3, the screen, the *Masach*, descends from its previous location, being the *Peh* of *Rosh*, to a lower level that will correspond to a force of desire equal to level 3. Remember the levels of *Keter* - Phase 0, *Hochma* - Phase 1, *Bina* - Phase 2, *Zeir Anpin* - Phase 3, and *Malchut* - Phase 4. Now when you refer back to figure number 4, those interior levels inside the *Toch* part of the *Partzuf* will become a bit clearer.

After the *Hizdakchut*, the withdrawal of the Light, the screen is lowered one level, one section. That means that the screen lowered to between the sections of *Keter* and *Hochma* in the *Toch*. This place in *Galgalta* is known as *Chazeh*, the place of level 3.

Now the whole process starts over. Once again the Light presses on the *Masach*, the screen, from above. The screen first rejects 100% of the Light as before. The creature then makes a calculation to accept some of the Light, but once again, only down to the *Tabur* of *Galgalta*. But remember, the screen has lowered a level, so there will be less Light entering. The process of *Hitpashtut* (expansion of Light) is happening again.

Once the Light reaches the *Tabur* (the navel), the screen begins to feel the pressure from both inside and out as before. The creature must get rid of the Light just like the first time. The screen rises, losing *Aviut* as it does. When the screen finally makes it back up to the *Rosh*, the head, new memories, *Reshimot*, fill the *Partzuf*. This time the levels are (3,2). Remember, that means the record of the Light has lowered one degree to level 3 *Hitlabshut* and the memory of the *Aviut* has lowered to level 2.

Just as before, the screen lowers to a level corresponding to its level of *Aviut* and the *Partzuf* shrinks once more. The screen is now at the level between *Hochma* and *Bina*, of *Galgalta* where the *Chazeh* exists in *AB*, the second *Partzuf*. This new *Partzuf* is known as SAG.

Once again the screen lowers and the same thing that happened in the first two *Partzufim* happens again. The screen rises back up to the *Peh* of the *Rosh* of SAG, and the *Reshimot* lower to (2,1). The new *Partzuf* created in the process is called MA. After the exact same process happens in MA, *Reshimot* of (1,0) come out from the *Hizdakchut* (withdrawal of Light) of MA and the final *Partzuf*, BON, is formed.

Each *Partzuf* consists of five parts: *Shoresh* - *Keter* (Root, 0), *Aleph* - *Hochma* (1), *Bet* - *Bina* (2), *Gimel* – *Zeir Anpin* (3) and *Dalet* - *Malchut* (4). There is not a desire you have ever had, currently have, or will ever have that does not contain these levels. No desire may appear without them. This formation is a rigid system that never changes.

This last level, *Dalet or Malchut*, feels all of the four previous desires. These desires are what the Creator used to create it. *Malchut* gives names to each of these desires and it is those names that describe how the creature perceives the Creator at any given moment.

This is exactly why the *Kli* is called by the name of the Creator: *Yod-Hey-Vav-Hey* – Y-H-V-H. What these letters represent, the desires we are made of, are studied at length in Kabbalah. They form something akin to the skeleton of a person. That person may be big or small, may be skinny or obese, but a person remains a person no matter what.

Now, before we end this lesson, let's clean up a few things. The *Partzufim* that are filled with the Light of *Hochma* are called *Galgalta* and *AB*. If they are filled with the Light of *Hassadim* (Mercy), they are called *SAG, MA,* and *BON.* All the different names of all the *Partzufim* are based on the combination of these two Lights that exist within a particular *Partzuf.* Every single thing written in Kabbalah as well as in the Torah is no more than spiritual *Partzufim* that are filled with either the Light of *Hochma* or the Light of *Hassadim,* or both, but in different ratios.

After the birth of the five *Partzufim: Galgalta, AB, SAG, MA,* and *BON,* all the *Reshimot* disappear. All the desires that could be filled with the Light, for the benefit of the Creator, have been exhausted. At this stage, the screen completely loses the ability to receive Light for the Creator and can only resist egoism without receiving anything.

So what happens here is that *Malchut* makes that First Restriction and then it can receive five portions of Light. You will remember that we spoke of the spiritual worlds. That first world mentioned, *Adam Kadmon,* is made up of the five *Partzufim* that were just created. *Malchut* has completed all five of its *Reshimot*

At first, in the World of *Ein Sof* (Infinity), *Malchut* was completely filled with Light. After that First Restriction, because of this system of *Partzufim,* it will now take in Light only up to the level of *Tabur.* Now *Malchut* must fill up the part that is below *Tabur,* called *Sof* (End) and spread Light all the way down to its *Sium* (Conclusion).

The Creator wants to fill *Malchut* with unlimited delight. All that is needed to achieve this is to create the conditions for *Malchut* to have the desire and the power to fill up the remaining part, or in other words: to send the delight back to the Creator.

LESSON 3

Certainly there are many new concepts in those first two chapters, and although a considerable effort has been made to simplify the material, you may be experiencing a feeling of being overwhelmed with new terms.For that reason, you may wish to review the first two chapters a couple of times. The material in the lessons is presented in a fairly technical and dry nature, but they are designed that way on purpose.

For those of you with that point in the heart demanding answers, and if you have an earnest desire for knowledge of this great Wisdom, that same desire that motivates you to further your efforts will also awaken what Kabbalah refers to as *Ohr Makif*. You might remember that this is Surrounding Light. This special Light further increases a student's desire to perceive the Creator. When the time is right, you will receive further help from a qualified teacher, as well as by working with others with the same burning desire inside them.

Now, let's get started again. We left off with the Light entering and leaving the *Partzuf*. What I am actually referring to here is a desire being fulfilled or unfulfilled. When the Light enters the *Partzuf*, this is the same as a desire being fulfilled, leaving us with a feeling of wholeness and delight. And when the Light leaves the *Partzuf*, the opposite happens and we feel frustrated, as if something is missing. This feeling comes to us even though there is no such thing as a feeling of emptiness or lack in the spiritual world.

So if pleasure, *Ohr Hochma*, exits the *Partzuf*, then *Ohr Hassadim* remains. When that pleasure (*Ohr Hochma*) is shoved out of the *Partzuf*, the *Partzuf* knows exactly what is going to happen by refusing that amount of pleasure. In other words, if it has a screen that rejects selfish enjoyment, it is replaced with *Ohr Hassadim*, or altruistic pleasure. This latter pleasure is far higher and stronger than selfish pleasure. Our task is to learn to sense that pleasure.

If the *Partzuf*, the soul, understands that it cannot receive under the condition of pleasing the Creator, but only to please itself, it will refuse the pleasure. It is quite obvious here that in order for it to actually make this decision, it must have some help. This help will come from an opposing force—something that has the power to reject the pleasure. That is precisely where the screen known as a *Masach* comes into play.

So if we have a screen to prevent Light from entering, the Vessel then begins to perceive the Light instead of only darkness. If there is no screen, then the Light simply enters. In such a state there is no opposition, and any perception is impossible. This would be similar to the flame of a candle that is nullified by the light of a torch. Another example might be a person with no eardrum. Without that screen inside the ear, all sorts of sounds may enter, but no hearing takes place. What causes the Vessel to be able to build a screen is the absence of the Light during the First Restriction performed by the Vessel.

We have a multitude of desires. But a desire can only be thought of as spiritual when a screen is placed at the entrance of the *Partzuf*. The screen operates as a sort of valve, allowing in that Light only under our primary condition of pleasing the Creator.

So our initial main objective is to receive that Light into the soul, the *Partzuf*. As soon as the Light enters the Vessel, it begins affecting it, transferring its own attributes to the Vessel. Once this happens, we feel the difference between our own properties (to receive) and the properties of the Light (to bestow). This process makes us feel ashamed of receiving the Light, and at the same time, makes us want to resemble the Light.

Now it is important to note here that Spiritual Light (pleasure from perception of the Creator) cannot change the nature of the Vessel from receiving to bestowing. It only has the ability to change for whom the Vessel receives pleasure, or the intent. Am I receiving because I want the pleasure for myself, or am I receiving in order to please the Creator?

If the Vessel chooses to use itself in this manner, it is called "receiving for the sake of giving." It is a situation where everybody wins. The Vessel, *Malchut*, gets to completely enjoy receiving the Light. At the same time, *Malchut* also returns delight to the Creator. This loop of pleasure is unending.

To explain this a bit further, let's go back to Phase 1 (*Hochma*). This is where the Direct Light (*Ohr Yashar*) enters the Vessel. *Malchut* received the pleasure from this *Ohr Yashar*. Of course, the sensation of the Giver cancels this Light. But in our condition where the Light extends all the way down to our world, and this time is returned using a screen, the *Masach*, *Malchut* does the same thing, fills up with all the Light, but this time its intent is to please the Creator. This allows it to reach endless Light. There is no cancellation. Thanks to this process, all its desires, both the lowest and the highest, lead to never-ending delight. This is also designated by the expression "feeling of completeness and unity."

Remember that we have five *Partzufim*, *Galgalta*, *AB*, *SAG*, *MA*, and *BON*. When *Galgalta* filled and then rejected the Light, *AB* was created and so on all the way to *BON*. But this is not nearly the end of the story. Remember that place called *Tabur* where it was impossible to receive Light in *Malchut*? Our goal is now to remedy that situation.

The problem is that the desires under *Tabur* do not have a screen, so they cannot be filled with Light. The good news is that there is just such a part of this spiritual machine that is designed to do that very thing. It is a new *Partzuf* called *Nekudot* of *SAG*. What does that mean? It means that *Partzuf Nekudot* is a sort of sub-*Partzuf* that comes out while the Light is exiting the *Partzuf SAG*. This *Partzuf* is unique and is actually able to go below *Tabur*, correcting all of those extremely powerful desires there as well.

In order to understand why, it is important to remember the names of the different *Partzufim*: *Galgalta* – *Keter*, *AB* – *Hochma*, *SAG* – *Bina*, *MA* – *Zeir Anpin*, and *BON* – *Malchut*. Remember Stage 3 called Phase *Bet*? In this stage the Vessel only wants to bestow, and that is the exact characteristic of *SAG*, called *Bina*. *Bina* could care less about receiving; it only wants to bestow, to give *Ohr Hassadim* without restraint, to be like the Creator. This makes it absolutely perfect for expanding below *Tabur* and dealing with those Vessels that cannot currently receive Light.

You might also remember that all *Partzufim* are built on memories (*Reshimot* or records) of the previous *Partzuf*. Also we have discussed that there are two kinds of *Reshimot*: *Reshimo* of the Light, called *Hitlabshut* and *Reshimo* of the desire, called *Aviut*. The breakdown is as follows: *Galgalta* is built on *Reshimot* (4, 4); *AB* is built on (4, 3); *SAG* is built on

(3, 2); MA is built on (2, 1) and BON is built on (1, 0). Now let's look at SAG. This *Partzuf* is built on a memory of pleasure (Light) with a strength of 3 and a memory of desire built with a strength of 2.

As the Light exits *Partzuf* SAG, it rises through those stages of a *Partzuf* we learned about (see figure 4). When the Light exits the interior *Bina* level of that *Partzuf*, the *Reshimot* that are left are (2,2), the exact combination of giving that is needed in order to lower beneath *Tabur*. And this is precisely what happens.

Below *Tabur*, the *Partzuf Nekudot* of SAG begins to expand and fill this section of *Galgalta* with the Light of *Hassadim*, the Light of Pleasure from giving. The entire purpose of this *Partzuf* is to elevate the uncorrected desires to its own level and correct them. It is important to remember that the whole purpose here is to correct the Vessel where it can receive everywhere, including the area below *Tabur*.

Below the *Tabur* in that place of the strongest desires, the *Nekudot de* SAG ("*de*" is Aramaic for "of") fill *Galgalta* with the Light of *Hassadim*, i.e. with the pleasures of giving. These pleasures can then be diffused without restraint to any desire in the *Partzuf*. Below the *Tabur*, the *Nekudot de* SAG form a new *Partzuf* which contains its own ten *Sefirot*: *Keter, Hochma, Bina, Hesed, Gevura, Tifferet, Netzah, Hod, Yesod* and *Malchut*.

This *Partzuf* bears the name of *Nekudot de* SAG. It is of paramount importance in the whole process of correction, since it is a part of *Bina*, which elevates the uncorrected desires to its level, corrects and raises above *Bina*.

From the top to the *Tabur*, *Galgalta* comprises:

i.   At the *Rosh* level: the *Sefirot Keter, Hochma* and *Bina*.
ii. At the *Toch* level: *Hesed, Gevura* and *Tifferet*.
iii. Below the *Tabur*, in the *Sof*: *Netzah, Hod, Yesod* and *Malchut*.

When *Nekudot de* SAG descend below the *Tabur* and begin to transmit the Light of *Hassadim* to the *Sof* of *Galgalta*, they are subjected to a strong reaction on the part of the *Reshimot* remaining in the *Sof* of

Galgalta from the Light that previously filled these *Kelim* (plural for *Kli*). You might remember that the very first thing the creature (Stage 4) does is completely take the Light in and fill *Galgalta*.

These *Reshimot* are of strength *Dalet-Gimel* (4,3). The strength of the *Dalet-Gimel* (*Hitlabshut* of level 4, *Aviut* of level 3) is higher than the strength of the *Masach* of the *Nekudot de SAG* (*Hitlabshut* of level 2, *Aviut* of level 2). Therefore SAG cannot oppose such a powerful Light-Desire and begins to desire to receive it for itself.

We can now examine the *Bina* phase in the spreading of the Direct Light from above downward (See Figure 6).

This phase is composed of two parts:

(i) In the first part, it does not want to receive anything, while giving without restraint. This part is called *Gar de Bina* and is endowed with altruistic attributes.

(ii) The second part already considers receiving the Light in order to transmit it further on. Although it is receiving, it does not do it for its own sake. This part of *Bina* is called *Zat de Bina*. The same thing occurs in the *Partzuf* of the *Nekudot de SAG*, which possesses the attributes of *Bina*:

The first six *Sefirot* bear the name of *Gar de Bina* and the last four *Sefirot* are named *Zat de Bina*. The powerful Light of *Hochma* that reaches *Gar de Bina* does not affect it; it is indifferent to this Light. This part of *Bina* wishes only to bestow. However, *Zat de Bina*, which desires to receive in order to give to the lower levels, may receive only that Light which relates to *Aviut Bet*.

If the desires reaching *Zat de Bina* are of a stronger *Aviut*, the desire to receive for oneself alone appears. In other words, *Bina* is divided into two parts, a part that only wishes to bestow no matter what, and another part that will receive, but only to pass Light to the parts below it. This means that *Zat de Bina* will only receive in order to pass that Light to the *Sefirot* below.

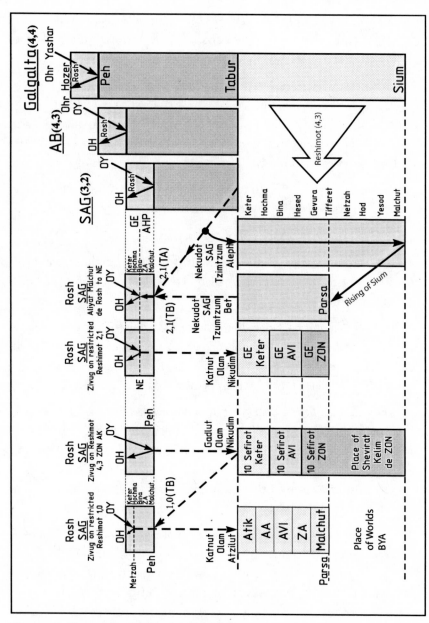

Figure 6. **Partzuf** of **Nekudot de SAG**

The problem here is that even though *Zat de Bina* only wants to receive in order to give, it will still receive. So when those massive desires below the *Tabur* appear, *Zat de Bina* cannot resist. But we have a restriction here that does not allow such reception. After the *Tzimtzum Aleph* (First Restriction), *Malchut* cannot receive with a self-aimed intention. Therefore, as soon as a desire of such strength appears in the *Zat* of *Nekudot de SAG*, *Malchut* rises and positions itself on the border between altruistic and selfish desires, in the middle of *Tifferet*, between *Gar de Bina* and *Zat de Bina*.

This act of *Malchut* is called *Tzimtzum Bet*, the Second Restriction. A new border for the spreading of the Light is being formed along this line: the *Parsa*. This border was located before in the *Sium* of *Galgalta*. While the Light was previously able to spread only down to the *Tabur*, even though it tried to penetrate under it, with the spreading of the *Partzuf* of the *Nekudot de SAG* below the *Tabur*, the Light of *Hassadim* did penetrate there, and paved the way for the spreading of the Light of *Hochma* to the *Parsa*.

A "place" is a *Sefira* (singular for *Sefirot*) inside of which another *Sefira*, smaller in dimension, can be fitted. An example of that is *Olam Nekudim*, inside of which are *Olamot* (worlds) ABYA (*Atzilut*, *Beria*, *Yetzira*, *Assiya*). Our world exists in a place. If you could take out absolutely everything the universe contains, then the place would remain. Our finite minds cannot perceive it, but this is simply a void that cannot be measured, since it is located in other dimensions. In addition to our world there exist spiritual worlds that are impossible to perceive or feel because they refer to other dimensions. Afterward, the World of *Atzilut* appears at the place of *Gar de Bina* below the *Tabur*. The World of *Beria* is formed under the *Parsa* in the lower section of *Tifferet*.

The World of *Yetzira* appears at the place of the *Sefirot Netzah*, *Hod*, and *Yesod*. The World of *Assiya*, whose last portion is called our world, is formed at the place of the *Sefira Malchut*.

How can ten *Sefirot* be obtained out of five: *Keter*, *Hochma*, *Bina*, *Zeir Anpin* and *Malchut*? *Zeir Anpin* is made up of six *Sefirot*: *Hesed*, *Gevura*,

Tifferet, Netzah, Hod, Yesod. If instead of *Zeir Anpin,* one places its six *Sefirot,* then along with *Keter, Hochma, Bina* and *Malchut,* ten *Sefirot* will be obtained. This is the reason why sometimes five or ten *Sefirot* are mentioned.

LESSON 4

For someone just being introduced to Kabbalah, the new terminology can at first be a bit overwhelming, but there is a purpose here. The reason the Kabbalistic terms have been kept is for readers who may wish to pursue further studies. Getting used to the terms now will make future efforts much more fruitful and save you quite a bit of time. Let's start Lesson 4 with a brief review of what we have learned.

Light initially emanating from the Creator in Phase 0, *Keter,* is the desire to give delight. This is the root phase of the process of creation. One can think of this phase as potential, similar to the thought of building a house. The house exists as potential in your mind. This Light brings forth the initial substance that will one day be the Creation, namely, the desire to receive delight. The creation of the desire to receive is called Phase 1, *Hochma.* One can think of it as the building of a Vessel and the filling of that Vessel with pleasure.

After the Vessel is filled with Light, it not only feels pleasure but also feels the attribute of the Giver. That attribute of the Giver is just that, the desire to bestow. Wishing not only to receive but to relate to the Giver as well, the Vessel adopts this attribute. This desire to relentlessly bring delight corresponds to Phase 2, *Bina.*

The creature has a problem here; it simply has nothing to give. But the creature also realizes that there is a way it can bring the Giver delight if it only accepts a portion of the Light for the sake of the Giver. This realization ushers in Phase 3, *Zeir Anpin.* Now our creature has two properties: to give and to receive.

What has actually happened here? The creature has actually perceived two kinds of delight. But in this phase, it feels that receiving is better than giving. This was its natural attribute, the initial character it had in Phase 1, *Hochma*. Next, the creature makes the monumental decision to receive all the Light, to be completely filled. The difference between this new Phase 4, *Malchut*, and Phase 1, *Hochma*, is that it made this decision totally on its own. In Phase 1, the Creator controlled everything.

Actually in the first three phases of creation (not counting Phase 0, the root phase), our creature is not really considered a creature. It is more of a creature in potential. Only in the last Phase, called *Malchut* of the World of *Ein Sof*, can our creature truly be considered a separate entity from the Creator. The key for this change in status was the creature's making its own independent decision.

The process of creation has now entered the fourth phase, called *Malchut* of the World of *Ein Sof*, the one and only true Creation. It combines the two conditions: it knows in advance what it wishes, and out of the two states, it chooses receiving. What the Creation has actually done is developed a sense of itself. It knows the Creator's attribute, and now it knows its own.

The difference between Phase 1 and Phase 4 may seem small, but actually it is a fundamental key that will have far-reaching and immense effects from Phase 4 on. The very fact that our creature has made a totally independent decision to accept all the pleasure for itself and is filled completely with the Light causes an incredible feeling of shame to arise. This feeling of shame is actually the feeling of the difference between what the creature feels as its own nature, and the nature of the Creator. Why did this not happen in Phase 1? Because the creature had no independent wish to receive pleasure; it was simply filled by the Giver. It had no way to compare their difference in properties.

This feeling of intense shame leads the creature to again make the decision to become like the Creator. The First Restriction, *Tzimtzum Aleph* now takes place. It is important to understand that this restriction was not made on the desire to receive pleasure, but on the intent to receive pleasure for self indulgence. In Phase 1, the creature simply stopped receiving. Here, the First Restriction means that the creature can most certainly receive pleasure, but not for its own sake.

The end result is that it can receive pleasure but only up to the point that it can receive for the sake of the Giver. That means its own strength of that intention is what rules whether it will receive or not. If the strength of its intention is weak, it can barely receive any Light at all. Yet if it has a strong intention not to receive for itself, then it can fill itself to just below the point where the intention can no longer be sustained.

We see that the receiving of Light only with the intent to benefit another is the same as bestowal. This is what separates our world from the spiritual world. There, everything is defined by the intention, not by any action. Here it is the exact opposite. It is also important to note that in the spiritual, there are no half measures. The First Restriction means that the creature will never receive delight for itself, period. The First Restriction has become a law and it is impossible to violate it.

The primary task of a created being is to neutralize the wish to receive delight for its own sake. The first created being, the creature in Phase 4 known as *Malchut,* shows how to receive pleasure from all of the Light of the Creator. But the First Restriction means that everything *Malchut* is filled with will never be received as delight for its own sake. We shall see how this principle can be further implemented.

You can think of *Malchut* after the First Restriction as a Vessel with a lid on it. Now that lid is replaced with a screen that pushes away all incoming Light. This first act happens every time, and every bit of the Light is rejected. Inside *Malchut,* there is a massive desire to receive that Light. In other words, *Malchut* initially places a screen above its egoism, which pushes away all the incoming Light. Yes, it does succeed in pushing away all the delight and does not luxuriate in it.

But there is still a problem here. The *Kli* (Vessel) is separated from the Light. So how can a situation be achieved where the delight is not simply pushed away, but some portion of it is received for the sake of the Creator? For this to take place, the Light reflected by the screen (*Ohr Hoz-*

er) must somehow clothe the Direct Light (*Ohr Yashar*) and together they will enter the *Kli*, the desire to receive. One can think of the screen as a type of valve, opening only under a certain condition. In our case, that condition is to accept the Light only to bring pleasure to the Creator.

Ohr Hozer serves as the anti-egoistic condition, a screen that accepts and allows in the *Ohr Yashar*, the delight, but only if it is receiving for the sake of the Creator. *Ohr Hozer* acts as an altruistic intention. Before taking in these two kinds of Light, a calculation is carried out in the *Rosh*, the calculating part of the soul. How much Light may be received for the Creator's sake? This quantity passes in the *Toch*.

The first *Partzuf* may receive, for example, 20% of the Light, according to the power of its screen. This Light is called Inner Light – *Ohr Pnimi*. The portion of Light that did not enter the *Kli* remains outside and is therefore called the Surrounding Light, *Ohr Makif*. The initial receiving of 20% of the Light is called *Partzuf Galgalta*.

Following the pressure of the two Lights, *Ohr Makif* and *Ohr Pnimi* on the Screen in the *Tabur*, the *Partzuf* expels all the Light. The screen then moves gradually up from *Tabur* to *Peh*, losing its anti-egoistic power and reaching the level of the screen in the *Peh de Rosh*.

It is very important to remember that nothing disappears in the spiritual world; each consecutive action encompasses the previous one. Thus, the 20% of Light received from *Peh* to *Tabur* remains in the previous state of the *Partzuf*.

Afterwards, seeing that it is not able to manage the 20% of Light, the *Partzuf* makes a decision to take the Light in again. This time it does not take in 20% of the Light, but only 15%. For this purpose, it has to lower its screen from the level of *Peh* to the level of *Chazeh* of the *Partzuf Galgalta*, thus moving down to a lower spiritual level.

If at the beginning its level was defined by the *Reshimot: Hitlabshut* of level 4 and *Aviut* of level 4, now it is only 4 and 3 respectively. The Light enters the same way and forms a new *Partzuf: AB*. The destiny of the new *Partzuf* is the same; it also pushes the Light away. Following on this occurrence, the third *Partzuf*, SAG, spreads out, and after it, MA and BON.

All five *Partzufim* fill *Galgalta* from its *Peh* to its *Tabur*. The world which they form is called *Adam Kadmon*. *Galgalta* is similar to Phase 0, *Keter*, since while receiving from the Creator it gives whatever it can. *AB* receives a smaller portion for the sake of the Creator, and is called *Hochma*, Phase 1. *SAG* works only for bestowal and is called *Bina*, Phase 2. *MA* is similar to *Zeir Anpin*, Phase 3, and *BON* corresponds to *Malchut*, Phase 4.

SAG, having the properties of *Bina* (only wanting to bestow), is able to spread under the *Tabur* and fill the lower part of *Galgalta* with Light of *Hassadim*. Thus, below the *Tabur*, with the exception of empty desires, remain the delights induced by similarity with the Creator.

All this happens because the *NHY* (*Sefirot: Netzah Hod Yesod*) part of *Galgalta* below the *Tabur* refused to take in the Light of *Hochma*. Remember that this is the Light of Reception. They enjoy the Light of *Hassadim*, the delight of similarity with the Creator, bestowing.

The *sub-Partzuf Nekudot de SAG* has *Aviut Bet*, and may enjoy from the bestowal of the Light only on this level. The *NHY* can no longer resist the delight of the level *Dalet*; otherwise they will begin to receive the Light for their own sakes.

The *NHY* should normally be able to receive, but *Malchut*, at the very bottom of *Galgalta* (*Sium* in Hebrew), rises to the middle of *Tifferet* of *Partzuf Nekudot de SAG* and forms a new *Sium* (Conclusion). This is the restriction of the Light, called *Parsa*, below which the Light cannot go. With this action *Malchut* makes the Second Restriction on the spreading of the Light, called *Tzimtzum Bet* by analogy with the first one.

To take an example from our everyday life: imagine a person with pleasant manners and good upbringing who would never steal up to the sum of $1000. However, if $10,000 were laid before that person, his or her education might not "work" because in this case, the temptation, the prospective delight, is too powerful to be resisted.

Tzimtzum Bet is the continuation of *Tzimtzum Aleph*, but on the Vessels of receiving, the *Kelim de Kabbalah*. These are the Vessels below *Tabur* with the desire of the strongest level – level 4. It is interesting to note that in the *Partzuf Nekudot de SAG*, the *Partzuf*, which is altruistic by nature, has disclosed its selfish properties; immediately *Malchut*, ascending upward, covers it and forms a line, called *Parsa*, to limit the downward spreading of the Light.

The *Rosh* of *Partzuf SAG*, as every Head, consists of five *Sefirot*: *Keter*, *Hochma*, *Bina*, *Zeir Anpin* and *Malchut*. These in turn are divided into the *Kelim de Hashpa'a* (Vessels of bestowal—*Keter*, *Hochma* and half of *Bina*) and *Kelim de Kabbalah* (Vessels of reception—from the middle of *Bina* to *Malchut*).

Kelim de Hashpa'a (Vessels of bestowal) are also called *Galgalta ve Eynaim* (GE). The *Kelim de Kabbalah* (Vessels of reception) are the *Awzen*, *Hotem*, and *Peh*: AHP (pronounced ah-hap). The restriction of *Tzimtzum Bet* means that from this point on, a *Partzuf* must not activate any of the Vessels of receiving. It is prohibited to use the *AHP*; so decided *Malchut*, when it rose to the middle of *Tifferet*.

After *Tzimtzum Bet*, all the *Reshimot* move up to the *Rosh* of SAG, there requesting to form a *Partzuf* exclusively on the level of the Vessels of bestowal. This allows the *Partzuf* to receive some Light from contact with the Creator.

It now means that the screen must be located not in *Peh* of the *Rosh*, but in *Nikvey Eynaim* of the *Rosh*, that part which corresponds to the line of *Parsa* in the middle of *Tifferet* in the *Guf*. Each part of the *Partzuf*, the *Rosh*, *Toch* and *Sof* has five levels of *Keter*, *Hochma*, *Bina*, *Zeir Anpin* and *Malchut*. The *Nikvey Eynaim*, which is the middle of *Tifferet* in the *Rosh*, corresponds to the Middle of *Tifferet* in the *Guf*. Remember *Gar de Bina* and *Zat de Bina*?

After a *Zivug* (coupling) in *Rosh* of SAG, a *Partzuf* will emerge from this point and will spread below the *Tabur* and down to the *Parsa*, that place *Malchut* rose to in the Second Restriction. The new *Partzuf*, which spreads below the *Tabur* to *Parsa*, clothes the previous *Partzuf* of *Nekudot de SAG*, but on its upper part only, *Gar de Bina*, meaning on altruistic *Kelim*, the Vessels of bestowal.

The name of the new *Partzuf* is *Katnut* of *Olam Nekudim* (Smallness of the World of *Nekudim*). This *Partzuf* appears on the level of the restricted *Reshimot* of *Bet-Aleph* (2,1). In fact, in the five worlds previously mentioned (*Adam Kadmon, Atzilut, Beria, Yetzira* and *Assiya*), such a world does not exist.

During the existence of this world, the *Sefirot Keter, Hochma, Bina, Hesed, Gevura* and the one third of *Tifferet* (the upper third) are divided into ten and have the usual names. In addition, there are special names for the *Sefirot Hochma* and *Bina: Abba ve Ima* (Father and Mother) and also, the *Sefirot Zeir Anpin* and *Malchut: Zeir Anpin* and *Nukva* (Female). When speaking of *Zeir Anpin* and *Nukva* together, they are called ZON. These additional names designate that these parts are from the world of *Nekudim*.

Following the *Zivug de Hakaa* in the *Nikvey Eynaim* in *Rosh* of SAG, upon the request of the *Reshimot* of the lower *Partzuf*, SAG performs a second *Zivug* on the *Reshimot* of *Gadlut* (Greatness) in the *Peh de Rosh*. In other words, SAG performs a *Zivug* on the level 4 of desire, the strongest level.

What has actually happened here? Remember that *Zivug* is a coupling of *Reshimo*. The *Nikvey Eynaim* is the dividing line between the section of pure bestowal and the section of Vessels that will receive but only in order to bestow in the *Rosh*. So the first thing that happens is a *Zivug* in what is called *Katnut* - only on Vessels of bestowal. The second *Zivug* is on greatness, or on all of the Vessels in the *Rosh*, both to bestow and Vessels that will receive in order to bestow.

As this second a *Zivug* takes place, a great Light begins to spread out from SAG and tries to descend below the *Parsa* where the massive desires are. *Partzuf Nekudim* is absolutely certain that it will be able to receive the Light for the sake of the Creator, and that it has enough power for this, notwithstanding the *Tzimtzum Bet*. But the moment the Light touches the *Parsa*, the *Shevirat ha Kelim* (breaking of the Vessels) occurs, because it becomes clear that the *Partzuf* wants to receive delight only for itself. Light immediately exits the *Partzuf* and all the Vessels, even those above the *Parsa*, are shattered.

So from the desire of the *Partzuf* to use the Vessels of reception for the Creator's sake, to form the World of *Nekudim* in *Gadlut*, using all ten *Kelim*, a shattering of all its screen-intentions occurred. In the *Guf* of the *Partzuf Nekudim*, i.e. in ZON above the *Parsa* (*Hesed, Gevura, Tifferet*) and below the *Parsa* (*Netzah, Hod, Yesod* and *Malchut*) there are eight *Sefirot*. Each of these consists of four phases (apart from Phase 0). These, in turn, bear ten *Sefirot*, yielding a total of 320 Vessels (4 x 8 x 10), which have been broken.

Of the 320 broken Vessels, only *Malchut* cannot be corrected and this represents 32 parts (4 x 8). The remaining 288 parts (320 - 32) can be corrected. The 32 parts are called *Lev ha Even* (lit. Heart of Stone). These will only be corrected by the Creator Himself at the time of *Gmar Tikkun* (End of Correction).

The altruistic and selfish desires have simultaneously broken apart and intermingled. As a result, every element of the broken Vessels consists of 288 parts that are fit for correction, and 32 that are not. Now the achievement of the goal of creation only depends on the correction of the broken World of *Nekudim*. If we succeed in our required task, Phase *Dalet* will be filled with the Light. *Olam ha Tikkun* (World of Correction) is created to build a coherent system, which will then correct the *Kelim* of the World of *Nekudim*.

This new world is also called World of Emanation, in Hebrew - *Olam Atzilut*.

LESSON 5

We have a total of 125 levels between us and the Creator. First there are the five worlds between the Creator and our world. These worlds are *Olam Adam Kadmon, Olam Atzilut, Olam Beria, Olam Yetzira*, and finally *Olam Assiya*. At the bottom end of *Olam Assiya* is our world.

Each world consists of five *Partzufim* (plural for *Partzuf*) called *Galgalta, AB, SAG, MA* and *BON*. Each *Partzuf* contains five *Sefirot* – *Keter, Hochma, Bina, Zeir Anpin* and *Malchut*. For *Malchut*, Phase 4 (*Dalet*), to reach the highest level, it must move through all of these levels. In this way *Malchut*, the only creation, merges with the four previous phases.

As *Malchut* rises through these levels, it fully absorbs all the properties in each phase and equalizes its attributes with the Creator's attributes. This is the Goal of creation. The very first thing that must happen now is that *Malchut* must be fully mixed with the other nine *Sefirot*.

For this task, a very special *Partzuf* is created. This *Partzuf* contains *Malchut* and the nine *Sefirot* from *Keter* to *Yesod*. Its name is *Adam ha Rishon*, or simply *Adam*. If you are wondering if this *Adam* is the same that is spoken of in Genesis of the Bible, it is most certainly one and the same *Adam*.

In the beginning, the nine *Sefirot* and the tenth, *Malchut*, are not connected to each other in any way. That's why it was said that in the beginning, *Adam* was forbidden to eat the fruit of the Tree of Knowledge of Good and Evil. With the fall of *Adam* and the breaking of his Vessels, the four upper phases (the nine first *Sefirot*), fall into *Malchut*.

All spiritual movements from above downward, from *Malchut* of *Ein Sof* to our world and back to the World of *Ein Sof*, are preordained. Nothing is planned that is not in accordance with the goal of creation. This goal is achieved when the fourth phase becomes similar to the third, second, first and zero phases, which are all contained in the fourth phases.

All the worlds appear as the descent of the Creator from above downward, over the 125 levels of the five worlds. This is like a permanent restriction of the Creator, making the whole of creation recede from Him until Creation reaches the level of our world, which no longer feels Him at all.

When creation rises upward, it makes its way through the same 125 levels of the five worlds that were formed for this specific purpose. Advancing a single level provides you with the power to take a leap forward to the next one.

The descent from above to below is the regression process of the soul, but the ascent is progression. During the descent, the power of each level lessens because it conceals more and more of the Light of the Creator from His creation. But the reverse movement increasingly reveals the Light of the Creator to us and grants us the power to overcome obstacles.

Let's take a look at what happens when the breaking of the Vessels (*Shevirat ha Kelim*) takes place in the world of *Nekudim*. The nine altruistic *Sefirot* that *Malchut*, being the selfish part, tries to use for her own sake, fall into *Malchut*. In the previous chapter we wrote that the *Zivug* (4,3) made in *Nekudim* caused the shattering of the Vessels. This *Zivug* was a request by *Malchut* for Light. *Malchut* wished to use the Light for its own pleasure, and the screen, having only the power of (2,2) could not possibly resist. At this time, altruism and selfishness are blended together as a result of the breaking, and we see this blending in our world as well.

An interesting point astute observers will immediately see is that the fall of *Adam* as told in the Bible was no accident. It was a necessity. Without that fall, there would have been no mixing of the attributes of the Creator with *Malchut*, and without that mixing there would have been no correction.

Now, if a strong Light enlightens this blend and awakens *Malchut*, making it understand its own nature and what the Creator is, *Malchut* can strive to be like the Upper *Sefirot*, i.e. the Light of the Creator. Even though the breaking of the Vessels seems to be an anti-spiritual action, actually it is the only possible process that can enable *Malchut* to bond with the altruistic properties of the Creator and to rise up to His level at a later stage.

After the breaking, two parallel systems of worlds, *Assiya*, *Yetzira*, *Beria*, and *Atzilut* are built as two systems: altruistic and selfish. These worlds are built on the basis of the breaking of the Vessels, which is why their system specifically grasps one's soul. The soul of *Adam* also consists of selfish and altruistic Vessels. The fall of *Adam* combined these two sorts of Vessels and his *Partzuf* was broken. When ascending to the appropriate level in the system of worlds, each broken part may discover its place there. .

Shevirat Neshamot (the breaking of souls) of *Adam* and *Shevirat Olam ha Nekudim* (breaking of the Vessels in the world of *Nekudim*) are built on the same basis. The worlds are a kind of outer casing for the soul. In our material world, it is the Universe, the Earth and everything around us, which forms the outer casing, enclosing mankind within it.

When examining how the World of *Atzilut* is designed, we may note that its structure completely matches the World of *Nekudim*. In fact, *Nekudim* is a model for *Atzilut. Partzuf Nekudot de SAG*, after *Tzimtzum Bet* (Second Restriction), ascends to the *Rosh* (Head) of *SAG* with three kinds of *Reshimot* (reminiscences).

From the restricted *Reshimot* of (2,1) *Bet-Aleph*, the World of *Nekudim* is formed in the *Katnut* (smallness) on *Kelim Galgalta ve Eynaim* (only on the Vessels of bestowal). This spreads downward from the *Tabur* (navel – the original border that divided the desires of *Aviut* level 4) to *Parsa*, that division in *Tifferet* that divides Vessels of bestowal and Vessels of reception.

This new *Partzuf*, like any other, is composed of *Rosh* and *Guf*. Its *Rosh* is divided into three parts: the first *Rosh* is called *Keter*, the second *Abba* (*Hochma*) and the third *Ima* (*Bina*). *Abba* literally means "Father" and *Bina* means "Mother" in Hebrew.

The *Guf* of the World of *Nekudim* is called ZON - *Zeir Anpin* and *Nukva*. Above the *Parsa* is *Gar de* ZON, below the *Parsa* we find *Zat de* ZON. *Gar de* ZON are Vessels of bestowal, *Zat de* ZON are Vessels of reception.

Following this, the World of *Nekudim* craved to enter the *Gadlut*, i.e., to join the *AHPs* to itself. Remember that *AHP* are Vessels of pure reception for oneself. *Nekudim* wants to correct these. But when the Upper Light reached *Parsa* and tried to cross it, the World of *Nekudim* broke apart.

Rosh Keter and *Rosh Abba ve Ima* remain, since the Heads do not break. But ZON, i.e., the *Guf*, breaks completely, both above the *Parsa*, and below it. Now, there are in total 320 broken parts, 32 of which (*Lev ha Even*) are not possible to correct by one's own power. The remaining 288 parts are subject to correction.

Next, in order to correct the broken Vessels, the world of Correction (*Olam ha Tikkun* also called *Olam Atzilut*) is created. *Reshimot* from the breakage of all 320 parts ascend to *Rosh* of SAG. At the beginning, the *Rosh* of SAG selects the purest parts, the lightest with respect to the ability to be corrected.

This is the Law of Correction: first the easiest parts get corrected and then with their help, the next parts are handled. Out of the corrected Vessels, *Rosh* of SAG creates the *Partzufim* of the World of *Atzilut*, similar to a small World of *Nekudim*:

(i)   Keter of the World of *Atzilut*, also named *Atik*
(ii) *Hochma*, also named *Arich Anpin*
(iii) *Bina*, also named *Abba ve Ima*
(iv) *Zeir Anpin*
(v)   *Malchut*, also named *Nukva*

The World of *Atzilut* is a replica of the World of *Nekudim*: *Atik* is located between the *Tabur* of *Galgalta* and *Parsa*; *Arich Anpin* from *Peh* of *Atik* to *Parsa*; *Abba ve Ima* from *Peh* of *Arich Anpin* to *Tabur* of *Arich Anpin*; *Zeir Anpin* stands from *Tabur* of *Arich Anpin* to *Parsa*; and *Malchut* is in the form of a point under *Zeir Anpin* (see Figure 7).

Each *Partzuf* is composed of two parts: *Galgalta ve Eynaim* (GE), Vessels of bestowal, and *AHP*, Vessels of reception. After being shattered, the Vessel consists not of two parts, but of four: GE, AHP, GE inside AHP and AHP inside GE. Such a combination can be found in each of the 320 broken Vessels. The goal here is to break each particle and separate the GE (Vessels of bestowal) from the AHP (Vessels of reception).

Here's how it works. The *Reshimot* of the corrected state cause the broken *Kelim* to draw *Ohr Makif*, which in turn separates the *Galgalta ve*

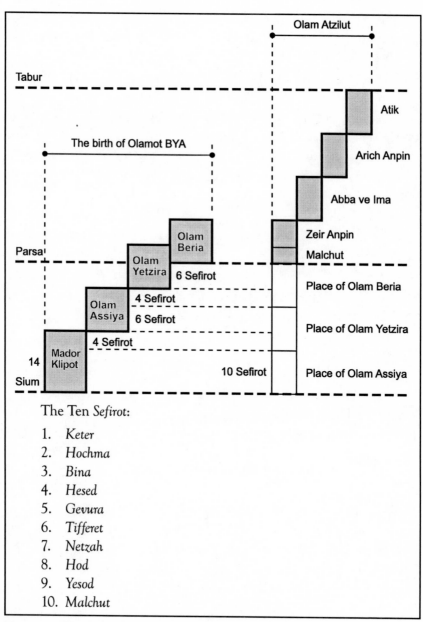

The Ten *Sefirot*:

1. *Keter*
2. *Hochma*
3. *Bina*
4. *Hesed*
5. *Gevura*
6. *Tifferet*
7. *Netzah*
8. *Hod*
9. *Yesod*
10. *Malchut*

Figure 7. The World of *Atzilut* and the Worlds of *BYA*

Eynaim from the *AHP* and elevates it to spirituality, while the *AHP* stays and awaits its turn for correction.

After the World of *Atzilut* corrects all the Vessels of bestowal, *Malchut* of the World of *Atzilut* ascends to *Bina*, i.e., under the *Rosh* of the World of *Atzilut*. The *Rosh* of the World of *Atzilut* are *Atik*, *Arich Anpin*, and *Abba ve Ima*. There *Malchut* performs the following actions:

(i) *Zivug* (coupling) on level 2 desire (*Bet de Aviut*), creating the World of *Beria*.
(ii) *Zivug* on level 1 desire (*Aleph de Aviut*), creating the World of *Yetzira*.
(iii) *Zivug* on level 0 desire (*Aviut Shoresh*), giving birth to the World of *Assiya*.

The ascent to *Bina* moves the World of *Atzilut* two levels up, which in turn moves everything under it up two levels. Everything moves together. *Malchut* is now in the place of *Abba ve Ima*, *Zeir Anpin* in the place of *Arich Anpin*, and *Arich Anpin* and *Atik* ascend in proportion. *Partzuf Malchut* of the World of *Atzilut*, which is in this ascent equivalent to *Bina*, to *Abba ve Ima*, can create, or "give birth."

The result of this ascent is that the World of *Beria* is born out of *Malchut* of *Atzilut* and occupies a new place instead of *Zeir Anpin* of the World of *Atzilut*, under the *Rosh*, that has given birth to it. The newborn is usually one level below its mother.

After this, the World of *Yetzira* is brought to life. Its first four *Sefirot*, i.e. its upper part, now occupy the place of *Malchut* of the World of *Atzilut*. In its lower part, six lower *Sefirot*, are located, correspondingly, in the position of the first six *Sefirot*, the place of the World of *Beria*.

The next world, *Assiya*, covers half of the World of *Beria* and half of the World of *Yetzira*. The four *Sefirot* of the World of *Yetzira* and the ten *Sefirot* of the World of *Assiya* remain empty. This empty place is called *Mador ha Klipot*, the Shell Section.

If you feel a bit confused about the last few paragraphs, realize that there is a difference between where these world's places were during their creation and where they are now. It will make it easier to find your way if you make full use of the figure above.

In order to emphasize its importance we can consider the whole process once more:

The World of *Nekudim* came out in *Katnut* with a *Rosh* having three parts, being *Keter* and the other two *Roshim* (plural for *Rosh*) being *Abba ve Ima*. ZON is its *Guf*. All this is called *Galgalta ve Eynaim* and spreads from *Tabur* to *Parsa*. After this, the *Gadlut* (Greatness) of the World of *Nekudim* begins to emerge, which has ten *Sefirot* both in *Rosh* and *Guf*.

Gadlut appeared in *Keter*, in *Abba ve Ima*, but when ZON wants to receive *Gadlut* the World of *Nekudim* breaks apart. It is important to remember that *Gadlut* is the spreading of Light not only to the Vessels of bestowal, but to the Vessels of reception as well. But the Vessels of reception have *Aviut* (strength of desire) of level 4, much greater than the screen. All of the *Kelim* of the *Guf* break into 320 parts; they fall under the *Parsa* and mingle with each other, yielding four groups:

(i)   *Galgalta ve Eynaim* (GE)
(ii) *AHP*
(iii) *Galgalta ve Eynaim* in *AHP*
(iv) *AHP* in *Galgalta ve Eynaim*

To correct the broken Vessels, the World of *Atzilut* is created. First, its three *Partzufim* are born: *Atik, Arich Anpin, Abba ve Ima*, which fully correspond to the *Partzufim*: *Keter* and *Abba ve Ima* in the World of *Nekudim*.

Zeir Anpin and *Malchut* correspond to the same *Partzufim* in the World of *Nekudim*. At this stage, the correction of the extracted Vessels of bestowal, *Galgalta ve Eynaim*, from all the 320 parts is finished. Further, we have *Galgalta ve Eynaim* inside the *AHP*.

Atzilut wants to do the correction in *AHP*. *Malchut* ascends to *Bina* and gives birth to the ten *Sefirot* of the World of *Beria*, which stands in place of *Zeir Anpin* of *Atzilut* because *Malchut* of the World of *Atzilut* is now in *Abba ve Ima*. Remember that *Zeir Anpin* was just below *Abba ve Ima*.

At this stage the ten *Sefirot* of the World of *Yetzira* are created; the last one partially overlaps the World of *Beria*. The part of the World of *Yetzira* is under *Parsa* in the place of the upper half of the World of *Beria*.

Finally, the World of *Assiya* is located from the middle part of the place of the World of *Beria* to the middle part of the place of the World of *Yetzira*. Beginning in the middle of the place of the World of *Yetzira* and finally ending in the place of the World of *Assiya* is emptiness, *Mador ha Klipot*.

Soon we will see that the worlds can ascend and descend, but always move together with respect to their initial position. All that we have discussed in this chapter is described in the 2100 pages of the *Talmud Eser Sefirot* (*The Study of the Ten Sefirot*) by Rav Yehuda Ashlag. You can imagine how encompassing this great work is, describing even the smallest of details. This most important work provides guidelines for our spiritual progression and helps keep us focused on the correct goal. It is no less than a blueprint for reaching the spiritual.

Our correction pertains to the Second Restriction, *Tzimtzum Bet*. As a result we cannot see beyond *Tzimtzum Aleph*, the First Restriction. Actually, there is no human way to even imagine the nature of reality that exists in that realm. These are referred to as "the secrets of the Kabbalah."

LESSON 6

As I have mentioned earlier, the World of *Atzilut* is quite similar to the World of *Nekudim*. The first *Partzuf* of the World of *Atzilut*, Atik, comes out on the *Reshimot* of *Aleph-Shoresh* (*Hitlabshut* of level 1, *Aviut* of level 0) in the *Katnut* (smallness) at first, from *Tabur* to *Parsa*. Then it spreads in the *Gadlut* (greatness) all the way to our world on the *Reshimot* of *Dalet-Gimel* (4,3).

It is the only *Partzuf* by means of which the Light can shine in our world. We do not see or feel this Light, but it shines and drives us forward. Whoever ascends from our world to below *Parsa*, where the worlds *Beria, Yetzira* and *Assiya* (BYA) are located, is called a righteous person, in Hebrew - *Tzadik*, a Kabbalist.

It is important to note that *Partzuf Atik* spreads not only to the *Parsa* in order to pass on Light to other *Partzufim* of the World of *Atzilut*, but below the *Parsa* as well. Since *Atik* is in *Tzimtzum Aleph*, this *Partzuf* is able to spread everywhere, and when it is below the *Parsa* it lights up the souls of the righteous who want to ascend to the World of *Atzilut*.

Being in the Worlds of BYA means "giving for the sake of bestowal," while being in the World of *Atzilut* means "receiving for the sake of bestowal." The next *Partzuf, Arich Anpin* (*Hochma*) comes out in *Katnut* (smallness - only Vessels of bestowal). After this *Partzuf, Abba ve Ima* (*Bina*) is born, then *Partzuf Zeir Anpin*, and finally *Malchut* is born in the form of a point. The AHPs of the five *Partzufim* of the World of *Atzilut* are the *Kelim de Kabbalah*, Vessels for receiving. The latter are to be restored and corrected.

The World of *Atzilut* is the only world we study. Our study of the other Worlds is limited only to the point by which they are related to the World of *Atzilut*. Our aim is to ultimately raise all the souls to *Atzilut*. *Partzuf Arich Anpin* wraps itself up with many different coverings, which are called *Se'arot*, or hair, similar to the hair of the human body.

The first three *Partzufim* of the World of *Atzilut* came out on the *Reshimot* of *Rosh* (Heads) of the World of *Nekudim*. *Zeir Anpin* of the World of *Atzilut* is called *Ha Kadosh Baruch Hu* (The Holy One Blessed Be He).

Malchut of the World of *Atzilut* is called *Shechina* - the aggregation of all the souls.

All the names, including the names of personages mentioned in the first five books of the Bible, spring from the World of *Atzilut*. And those personages in the Worlds of BYA are all the same under the control of the World of *Atzilut*.

The World of *Atzilut* does not let through any Light below the *Parsa* apart from a tiny ray of Light called *Ohr Tolada*. This minute Light is what allows us to feel the tiny pleasures we feel in this world. How are the *AHPs* that are located below the *Parsa* corrected? They are illuminated with a powerful Light by which they see how they differ from the Creator.

They then wish to improve themselves and apply to the *Partzuf* located above, which is the Creator for them. They ask for the feature of bestowal, or a *Masach* (screen). If the request coming from the *AHP* is authentic, the *Partzuf* located above lifts it out of the Worlds of *BYA* and into the World of *Atzilut*.

The filling with Light only takes place in the World of *Atzilut*. *AHPs* in the Worlds of *BYA* are actually the seven *Sefirot* of *Zeir Anpin* and the nine lower *Sefirot* of *Malchut* of the World of *Atzilut*. This is because the Vessels of bestowal (*Galgalta ve Eynaim*) of *Zeir Anpin* and the *Sefira* (singular for *Sefirot*) of *Keter* of *Malchut* are in the World of *Atzilut*.

The request for help ascends to *AHPs* of *Zeir Anpin* and *Malchut*, located in the Worlds of *BYA*. If these *Sefirot* can be lifted and attached to the corresponding *Sefirot* of the World of *Atzilut*, then it will be possible to fill them with Light. Such a condition is called *Gmar Tikkun* (End of Correction).

So what is the difference between the ascending *AHP* (Vessels of reception) and those which are reached by the Light coming below the *Parsa*? The difference is qualitative: when the *AHP* goes up, it is used as a Vessel for bestowal, not for receiving. Its main feature of receiving is removed during the ascension.

In other words, instead of being used as a Vessel of reception (*AHP*) it is used as *Galgalta ve Eynaim* (Vessels of bestowal). This adds something to the World of *Atzilut*, but does not correct the *AHP* fundamentally. While ascending, the *AHP* does not use its own Light, but the Light of *Galgalta ve Eynaim*.

In addition to *AHPs* that can be raised to the World of *Atzilut,* there are many *Kelim* (Vessels) left in *BYA* that cannot be raised. This is because they are not combined with *Galgalta ve Eynaim.* What can be done in order to correct these *Kelim?* Just like the *Shevirat ha Kelim* (breaking of the Vessels) in the worlds, a *Shevirat ha Kelim* in the souls is produced.

For this purpose, *Malchut* of the *Ein Sof* (nothing more than a pure-ly selfish created being, devoid of altruism and in a state of restriction that it accepted on itself) is added to the Vessels of *Galgalta ve Eynaim* of the *ZON* of the World of *Atzilut.*

Here there will be such a combination of *Kelim de Kabbalah* (ves-sels of reception) with *Kelim de Hashpa'a* (vessels of bestowal) that natu-rally, such a *Partzuf* will break into smaller particles. Further, the separate sparks of altruism and selfishness will combine, paving the way for the correction of *Malchut* by means of these same particles.

And so, after the World of *Atzilut* enters the state of *Katnut, Mal-chut* of the World of *Atzilut* ascends to the level of *Ima* (*Bina*) of the World of *Atzilut* and there gives birth to the World of *Beria,* by making a *Zivug* on *Aviut Bet* (level 2).

After the second *Zivug* of *Malchut* on the *Aviut Gimel* (level 3), the World of *Yetzira* is born. Then the World of *Assiya* is brought about after the third *Zivug* of *Malchut* on the *Aviut Dalet* (level 4). After all this, a fun-damentally new *Partzuf* is being created in *Katnut* with *Galgalta Eynaim,* the Vessels of bestowal. The *AHP* of this new *Partzuf* in the future *Gadlut* will be *Malchut* of the *Ein Sof* itself.

This *Partzuf* is called *Adam ha Rishon* (First Man). But why were these additional Worlds of *BYA* created? This is to build the necessary environment for this *Partzuf,* wherein it would exist and receive from all around the required Light, to match its ever changing desires. As in the World of *Nekudim,* the *Partzuf* of *Adam ha Rishon* is born in *Katnut* with *Kelim Galgalta ve Eynaim.*

Similar to all *Partzufim*, it wishes to enter to *Gadlut*. But the moment it starts to receive Light for *Gadlut*, in the *Kelim de Kabbalah* (*AHP*) of *Malchut* of the *Ein Sof*, it breaks up into small particles.

When *Adam* was born, he was absolutely righteous (a *Tzadik*), he was already circumcised (his Vessels were of pure bestowal), and devoid of *Kelim de Kabbalah*. Then, as he developed, he wanted to correct the whole Garden of Eden, i.e., all his desires. This, in spite of strict instructions from the Creator not to do *Zivug* on *Malchut* of *Malchut* (those are the bad boys, the strongest desires to receive only for ourselves), which is unable to absorb altruistic intentions, any *Kelim de Hashpa'a*.

Adam had no qualms about his capacity to perform a correction on *Malchut* of the *Ein Sof*, because it was his own *AHP*. But the moment Light began to descend from the World of *Atzilut* below the *Parsa*, *Adam ha Rishon* was shattered into 600,000 parts.

Each of these parts has to spend 6,000 years (6,000 stages of correction) striving to accomplish its individual correction. The part of selfishness that one corrects to similarity with the Creator is called "the soul." In the instant of breaking up, all the desires of *Adam* fell down to the lowest level of selfishness. At this point all the fragments are separated, and each separate particle strives to draw pleasure and delight from this world.

This explains why special conditions were established to help one strengthen one's bonding with the Creator and to receive the correcting Light from above. While undergoing correction, one must send a request to the Creator for assistance to correct all desires. The Light of the Creator comes down, and 6,000 consecutive actions must be taken to correct the soul.

When this happens, the soul becomes similar in its attributes to *Malchut* of the *Ein Sof*. It then receives all the Light for the sake of the Creator. Everything we discover relates to the World of *Atzilut* and to the *Partzuf* of *Adam ha Rishon*.

All that is written in the Kabbalah concerns some part of this *Partzuf* or the world in which it comes out. The perception of the surrounding world at any given time depends on how high a level a person has risen to, and which part of the *Partzuf* of *Adam ha Rishon*. In order to bond with the spiritual world, we must achieve a similarity of attributes with that world.

If even one desire matches the spiritual attribute of giving relentlessly, then at this stage, a connection with the Creator is established. However, it is quite difficult to establish this first contact. When we open up to the spiritual, we clearly comprehend it and cannot mistake it. We then need to transform our desires. The Creator, for His part, wants us to achieve correction and awaits our request.

The divine Light exists in an absolute stillness—only the souls are transformed. At every stage of the transformation they receive new information from the Light. The Creator only replies to sincere prayer/desire. If He does not answer, it means that this is not yet a true desire to be answered. When we are ready, the answer will come immediately because the Light always wants to fill the *Kli*.

LESSON 7

The birth of the five worlds—*Adam Kadmon, Atzilut, Beria, Yetzira,* and *Assiya*—is actually the realization of the five *Sefirot: Keter, Hochma, Bina, Zeir Anpin,* and *Malchut,* which were in *Malchut* itself. The spreading of the worlds from Above to Below matches the progressive increase of the *Aviut* of the four desires or phases from 0 to 4.

The worlds are like a sphere surrounding *Malchut*. As an analogy, picture a person surrounded by concentric spheres and using his or her organs of sensation to perceive only the sphere closest to them: the World of *Assiya*. By sharpening our organs of sensation and by modifying his qualities, we gradually begin to perceive the next sphere, and so on.

All the worlds are a sort of filter placed in the Light's path, a special screen that blocks the Surrounding Light: the *Ohr Makif*. As soon as one senses the presence of these worlds, one removes the "screen-filters." This draws one closer to the Creator.

If the Light reached us without being filtered, it would bring about the *Shevirat ha Kelim* of our Vessels. By removing all "screen-worlds" we allow all the worlds to penetrate us. At this stage we acquire the Light and possess attributes similar to those of the Light. Such a state of being is associated with *Gmar Tikkun* – the End of Correction.

In the beginning, we as creatures are located inside the worlds and perceive their power and the constraints imposed upon us. How can we overcome these constraints? By performing an inner correction, corresponding, for instance, to the attributes of the World of *Assiya*. This means being an altruist on level zero.

When we acquire the attributes of zero level altruism, the World of *Assiya* penetrates us and can then be sensed by us. In order to sense the World of *Yetzira*, we must acquire attributes similar to those of this world and to allow this world to penetrate us. At this stage we become level 1 altruists. Our goal is to let all the worlds in, and to become similar to these worlds according to the following degrees of *Aviut*: 2, 3, 4.

By this means, *Malchut* is fully corrected and absorbs the first nine *Sefirot*, while we move beyond the limits of all the worlds and reach the World of Infinity (*Olam Ein Sof*). To begin correction, we need to recognize our own attributes, as well as aspire to the attributes of the Creator.

Each new *Partzuf* of the World of *Atzilut* starts from the *Peh* of the previous *Partzuf*, except for the *Partzufim* of Zeir Anpin and *Malchut*; *Zeir Anpin* starts from the *Tabur* of Abba ve Ima and *Malchut* starts from the *Tabur* of Zeir Anpin.

The three *Partzufim* of Atik, Arich Anpin, and Abba ve Ima are called *Keter*, *Hochma* and *Bina*, which correspond to *Keter*, *Hochma*, and *Bina* of the World of *Nekudim*. The *Rosh* of the World of *Atzilut* corresponds to the two Heads of the World of *Nekudim* and fulfills the same function. The *Rosh* of the World of *Atzilut*, which consists of *Atik*, *Arich Anpin*, and *Abba ve Ima*, was the first to emerge on the *Reshimot* of the non-broken *Kelim* of the World of *Nekudim*.

However, *Zeir Anpin* and *Malchut* are gradually restored. Only *Gal-galta ve Eynaim* are restored from *Zeir Anpin* and a single point from *Malchut*. The *AHPs* of *Zeir Anpin* and *Malchut* are in the Worlds of *BYA*. If these *AHPs* are corrected, then all worlds are corrected. The correction is carried out with the help of the *Partzuf* of *Adam ha Rishon*.

What is this *Partzuf* of *Adam ha Rishon* like? *Malchut* of the World of *Atzilut* is raised to the level of *Bina*. This is achieved in three phases. The whole World of *Atzilut* then ascends three levels. The normal condition of the World of *Atzilut* is called "a weekday." During such days the World of *Atzilut* is illuminated by an incomplete Light, which spreads down to the *Parsa*.

After this, a greater Light comes down from Above and grants higher attributes to the World of *Atzilut*, making it move up one level. Now *Malchut* is located in the place of *Zeir Anpin*. *Zeir Anpin* now reaches the level of *Abba ve Ima*. *Abba ve Ima* replaces *Arich Anpin*, which in turn rises to the level of *Atik*, which finally rises even higher into *SAG*.

The first elevation of the World of *Atzilut* takes place on Friday evening, *Erev Shabbat*. Such a progression is called "awakening from Above," (Aramaic: *Itaruta de La'ila*). In our world this corresponds to days, weeks, time and all that is not dependent on us, but is dependent on the laws of nature over which we have no control.

The next phase elevates the World of *Atzilut* one level higher. *Malchut* now stands on the level of *Abba ve Ima*, where it is endowed with an additional attribute: the intention to give. At this stage *Malchut* may receive for the Creator's sake. It now has a screen and is able to perform a *Zivug de Hakaa*, thus creating new *Partzufim*. Based on the attributes of *Abba ve Ima* on the one hand, and on the attributes of the *Malchut* of the *Ein Sof*, on the other hand, *Malchut* creates a new *Partzuf*: *Adam ha Rishon*.

For a Kabbalist, spiritual states, called *Erev Shabbat* (Friday evening), *Shabbat* (Saturday), *Motzei Shabbat* (Saturday evening) may be experienced on days bearing no connection to the calendar. For a Kabbalist, six days may last a split second, while *Shabbat* may last several days.

Everything that occurs in this world relates to our bodies, but what takes place in the spiritual world relates to the soul. For the time being, we can witness that our soul and body are not synchronized. But in the future, our world will operate with the same principles as those of the spiritual worlds, which will happen when the *Gmar Tikkun* is achieved. Then, all the deeds of the two worlds, as well as all the times, will merge.

If you have changed and the change has taken you one second, and your next change takes five years, then this means that your next second will have lasted five years. In the spiritual world, time is measured by the transformation of our attributes. A thousand years may elapse in our world before one begins to study Kabbalah. Upon entering the spiritual, we are able to live in a day what we used to live in several lives. This is an example of transformation and the shrinking of time.

Spiritual years correspond to the 6,000 degrees, levels of BYA and they cannot be matched with our material time referential. Ascent from the Worlds of BYA to the World of *Atzilut* is called *Shabbat* (Saturday). The portion ranging between *Tabur* of *Galgalta* and the *Parsa* is called *Shabbat*.

The first ascent is the ascent of the World of *Beria* to the World of *Atzilut*, the second one is the ascent of the World of *Yetzira* to the World of *Atzilut*, and the third relates to the World of *Assiya*. The ascent of the Worlds of BYA and the World of *Atzilut* takes place simultaneously.

When the third phase of ascent occurs, the World of *Atzilut* encompasses the *Zeir Anpin* and the *Malchut* of *Atzilut* and the Worlds of BYA. At this time the *Rosh* of the World of *Atzilut*: *Atik, Arich Anpin, Abba ve Ima*, duly cross the boundaries of the World of *Atzilut* and enter the World of *Adam Kadmon*. The *Rosh* of *Galgalta* ascends in its turn (Phase 1 of the ascent) together with *Rosh AB* (Phase 2 of the ascent), and with *Rosh SAG* (Phase 3 of the ascent) and enters the World of *Ein Sof*.

The direction of spiritual time is always from the bottom up. All souls, all of mankind, without being aware of the process, are constantly ascending, getting closer to the Creator in order to bond with Him. This is called "the direct flow of spiritual time." Time is always measured in the positive direction, even if we experience the process as negative.

We are egoistic, which is why the spiritual is perceived as negative. However, we never degrade ourselves when we walk the path of spiritual progress. In this world we should not seek to inflate our ego. Rather, we should long to come closer to the Creator. While working towards this goal, and until we complete our correction, we will increasingly sense our growing egoism. In other words, our natural egoism will seem worse compared to His divine attributes.

The correct study of Kabbalah attracts the Surrounding Light (*Ohr Makif*) whose function is to disclose one's true attributes. These appear ever more negative, albeit they have remained unchanged. In fact, one has only become more aware of the true nature of one's attributes under the influence of the divine Light. This awareness reveals that we have made progress, even if we feel otherwise.

What are the Worlds of BYA like? They are the altruistic *Kelim* which have fallen into the *AHP* below the *Parsa*. These worlds are also divided into *Galgalta ve Eynaim* and *AHP*. Their *Galgalta ve Eynaim* end in the *Chazeh* (Chest) of the World of *Yetzira*, i.e. after the ten *Sefirot* of the World of *Beria* and the six *Sefirot* of the World of *Yetzira*.

The fourteen lower *Sefirot* from the *Chazeh* of *Yetzira* and below (four *Sefirot* of the World of *Yetzira* and ten *Sefirot* of the World of *Assiya*) are the *AHP* of the Worlds of BYA. The World of *Atzilut* illuminates with its Light the Worlds of BYA all the way down to the *Chazeh* of the World of *Yetzira*. The World of *Atzilut* is called *Shabbat*.

The sixteen upper *Sefirot* of the Worlds of BYA (*Galgalta ve Eynaim*), from the *Parsa* to the *Chazeh*, are called the "*Shabbat* boundary" (*Tehum Shabbat*) but the World of *Atzilut* itself is called *Ir* (city). Even when all the Worlds of BYA ascend to the World of *Atzilut*, it is still possible to work with desires located below the *Parsa* up to the *Chazeh* of the World of *Yetzira* (*Galgalta ve Eynaim*).

That is why in our world, it is allowed during *Shabbat* to cross the limits of the city, but only in the limits of the city within the boundaries of *Tehum Shabbat*. This distance is measured as 2000 *Ama* (approximately 3000 feet) and 70 *Ama*. How is this distance divided?

From the *Parsa* to the *Chazeh* of the World of *Beria* it is called *Ibur* and equals 70 *Ama*. This distance is included in the World of *Atzilut* even though it is located outside it. It is an outer strip surrounding the city. The distance from the *Chazeh* of the world *Beria* to the *Chazeh* of the World of *Yetzira* equals 2000 *Ama*.

The whole distance between the *Parsa* and the *Sium* is 6,000 *Ama*. The portion of the Worlds of BYA stretching from the *Chazeh* of *Yetzira* to the *Sium* is called "Shell Section" - *Mador ha Klipot* (the place of the Husks). This *Mador ha Klipot* is composed of the *AHPs* of the Worlds of BYA, which embrace the four *Sefirot* of the World of *Yetzira* and the ten *Sefirot* of the World of *Assiya*. It is a place absolutely devoid of sanctity (*Kedusha*). One cannot go there during *Shabbat*.

The souls are lifted to the World of *Atzilut* to show them what inherent limits exist there, so that they can keep within them. When we set ourselves limits, we do not notice them. We are above these limitations, and they are not constraining us. Then the actions we undertake stem from our own attributes. The goal of creation implies a personal ascent, and *Shabbat* exists in order to show us what exists in the Higher Worlds, what there is to strive for.

Correction is achieved when the Light of the Creator shines directly, no longer through the worlds that act like filters. The shining of the Light is unbounded and brings unbridled delight to fulfill the goal of creation.

LESSON 8

To summarize what we have covered so far:

There are five filters around us that conceal the Light of the Creator, or five worlds. If we act naturally, for ourselves, we find ourselves under the influence of these filters. All of them are above us. If one decides to correct oneself in accordance with the properties of just one of these filters, even the lowest of them, that person will ascend. He or she will stand above the filter and their attributes will match the attributes of the given world. Furthermore, if that person's attributes become similar to those of the other two worlds, he will neutralize the action of these two filters as well, and will find himself above them.

We are now experiencing *Tzimtzum*, and it seems to us that the Creator no longer wants us to perceive Him, which is why He conceals Himself. Actually, if we perform a correction equal to the World of *Assiya*, this means we are located in this world. We have removed the filter we no longer need as we can now retain the Light and receive it for the sake of giving. Then we realize that for the Creator it does not matter whether we are making the restriction in order to receive for His sake or for our own.

Simply, the individual reaches a level where there is no distinction between receiving or giving, truth and lies, good deeds and transgressions. We choose what we prefer. But on the Creator's side there is only one desire, to delight us. The type of delight depends on the receiver.

The main objective is, without any conditions set by the Creator, to choose the altruistic ascent even though no reward or punishment for self will be incurred. This choice is not on the punishment-reward level, but is on the highest spiritual level where selflessness and detachment prevail.

The Creator places five filters in front of us to seal us off from the divine Light. Behind the fifth and final filter, the Creator is not sensed at all. This is where our material world is located. There also, life is supported by a tiny spark of Light (*Ner Dakik*), which is the meaning of our life, the sum of all our desires from all generations, in all souls, since the dawn of mankind.

This Light is so minute that the deeds carried out by the souls are not considered transgressions, but are merely considered as minimal animal life. There is no restriction on receiving these minimal pleasures. So live and enjoy...

However, if you want more, you have to become similar to the spiritual. Each spiritual pleasure means committing a completely altruistic bestowal, regardless of yourself. To achieve this, you must reach a certain level and act like the filter itself, by shielding away the incoming Light.

The filter then ceases to exist, and one is able to push away the Light that strives to enter one's *Kli*. This person will later on receive, but for the sake of the Creator. The soul of *Adam* conformed to the 30 *Sefirot* of the three Worlds of *BYA*, which represent the same World of *Atzilut*, but are located inside egoistic desires with *Aviut Bet*, *Aviut Gimel*, and *Aviut Dalet*.

When *Adam* corrects his actions and spiritualizes them, he ascends together with the worlds to the World of *Atzilut*. After passing through the 6,000 degrees of correction, *Adam ha Rishon* fully ascends to the World of *Atzilut*. Each soul, being a fragment of the *Partzuf* of *Adam ha Rishon*, follows the same path.

We cannot choose what needs to be corrected, but correct what is sent to us from Above, what is revealed to us. And so on to the Highest level.

CHAPTER 9.
THE LANGUAGE OF KABBALAH

Like any other science, in order to study Kabbalah, one must be aware of the language and terms. If I open up a book on particle physics, I am going to see terms like quarks, hadrons, gluons, flavors etc. Unless I have some reasonable definitions of what these words mean, I will be lost. So before we dive into the spiritual worlds and how they came into existence, let's take a look at the language of Kabbalah along with some definitions.

GOD

By "God," we usually refer to a higher power in general, the design of creation as it is expressed at any level. Any definition of something higher than you, the Creator, God, etc., relates to the feeling inside the creature. Since we cannot possibly feel anything outside ourselves, these definitions are always subjective.

FUNDAMENTAL CONCEPTS: A FRAMEWORK

Here are some common Kabbalistic terms that we relate to our corporeal world as well.

LIGHT

Light is perception of the Creator. There is only one Light and that does not change. But it is perceived in various forms due to differing states of the Vessels (the creature, the soul) – depending on the Vessel's ability to receive. From this we learn that we have no concept of the Light that is outside the Vessel, because we cannot define something that is out of our sensation.

Light is the sensation of the Creator by the creature; what stems from the Creator; something that we feel as good, whereas we feel its absence as bad. The Light that is spoken of in the first day of the creation of the world is the uppermost Light, which includes everything in it. The rest of the Lights are but derivatives of it, particular manifestations of it.

Concept	Definition
Time	In spirituality, time does not exist! Creation is eternal.
Creator	The desire to delight the creature. (see "God" above)
Creature, Soul	The desire to delight in the Creator, in the sensation of the Creator, in the Light.
Life	The fulfillment of the soul by the Light, the sensation of the Creator.
Death	The exit of the Light, the disappearance of the sensation of the Creator from the soul (as a result of the disappearance of the intent for the Creator)
The reception of a soul	An acquisition of intent (to enjoy for the Creator), with which it is possible to sense the Creator.
Masach (Screen)	The desire to enjoy with the intent for the Creator; the Holy Vessel, the spiritual Vessel, the corrected Vessel; the Vessel of the soul, which can feel the Creator.
Kabbalah (Reception)	The science that explains how to gradually receive a complete soul, meaning complete adhesion with the Creator.
Our World	A state lower than spiritual death, below the sensation of the Creator. Located under the left side of the impure worlds of *ABYA* (*Atzilut, Beria, Yetzira, Assiya*).
The birth of the soul, acquisition of life	A passage from the sensation of our world to the sensation of the Creator.
Reincarnation, cycles of life and death	The constant entrance and exit of Light in the Vessel of the soul, which continues throughout the correction in the worlds of *BYA*.

SPIRITUAL

Spiritual is that which is above our world. That which is absolutely not for me, but only for the Creator, when the outcome of the act is not related in any way to the one who performs it, even indirectly.

The soul is linked with the Creator, senses it and is filled by it, at least in the smallest amount. It is anything that is out of and above time, space and motion, which is not in any way linked with the sensation of the animate body, but is felt in some inner space in one's senses - intended for the Creator only - and revealed only when one is in control of the spiritual barrier.

The spiritual is not a component of our world. The spiritual is *in it*, but it does not appear in it directly, but rather through "clothing." Our world is a state where the will to receive enjoys only a very small Light, called "minute Light," and we can enjoy it even when the aim of the desire is for me.

The Creator does this purposely. We can enjoy that tiny Light, although we have not yet acquired a spiritual intent to give to the Creator, and do not have a screen. The will to enjoy that is found within us is the smallest of the created desires. It is separated from all other desires of the soul, so that we may practice on it, and finally reach admittance to the spiritual world.

Baruch Ashlag compared it to how children were taught to write in the old days: pen and paper were too expensive, so children would be given a piece of chalk and board to write on, so that they would not waste precious paper, until they learned to write correctly.

The term, *Klipot*, or Shells, are impure forces that are above our world. They do not exist in a normal person and appear only when a genuine desire for the Creator begins to emerge. In order to intensify that desire, negative forces are incited. By resisting them, we increase and intensify are desire for the Creator. They were created specifically for that - to interrupt and produce doubts.

Although the *Klipot* do not exist in our world, we still do not define them as "spiritual." They exist inside us and not outside us, and serve as a means and aid on our path to the Creator - a "help against ourselves." As strange as it may seem, these negative forces push us toward the Creator.

GIMATRIA

In order to describe various situations of the soul, we tend to use a name that is specifically adapted to its spiritual level, instead of using many technical details. All the Vessels (souls) consist of ten *Sefirot*, and one's body consists of 613 parts.

The Light that fills souls is what differentiates them from one another. The purpose of the name is to express attributes of the soul that is filled with Light. The sum of the Lights, or better put, the ten Lights that fill the ten *Sefirot* of the soul, are called *Gimatria*. That is why it is no more and no less than a recording of the spiritual situation of the soul and its fulfillment with Light by the Creator.

That Light depends on a screen: the attribute of the soul to give vs. its will to receive. The screen can only be acquired by the method of correction called Kabbalah.

REPENTANCE

Repentance is the return of the soul to the Creator, the place where it came from into this world. In the beginning, the Creator created a desire to receive. That desire was created without intent and was therefore called a "root."

By a gradual intensification of the aim for me, the desire to receive moves farther and farther from the Creator until it is completely opposite to Him. The state where all the desires aim for me is called "our world," or "this world." In that situation, the desire feels nothing but itself, and that sensation is called "body" (a person in this world).

If the desire changes its intent from for me to for the Creator, then the change in the intent causes the desire to return to its preliminary situation, and it becomes like an embryo in the Creator. Each situation in the spiritual realm is measured against the Creator and is determined in relation to Him. The more the attributes of the creature equalize with those of the Creator, the nearer in nature to the Creator is the creature regarded, and vice versa.

With the aim, for the Creator, the desire changes its quality and changes from being a *receiver* into being a *giver*. In this way, it equalizes with the Creator. The creature feels itself not as before – a point, or an embryo – but as something complete and whole and equal to the Creator. In its equivalence with the Creator, the will to enjoy senses everything the Creator senses: unbounded pleasure, eternity, and perfection. That is the purpose of creation.

LIFE AND DEATH

The sensation of death or life begins with the admittance to the spiritual world, and not when a physical body is born or dies. "Death" is an exit of Light when the sensation of the Creator is gone from the Vessel, the soul. Our present state is considered worse than death because we don't feel the Creator whatsoever. We do not even feel that we are denied of any Light, any sensation of the Creator. Feeling the Creator means receiving a soul, the awakening of that point in the heart in each of us.

The word, Kabbalah, is derived from the word, *Lekabel* (to receive). Kabbalah is the science that teaches how to receive a soul and, through it, to attain eternal life. "Death" means distancing from the Creator to its opposite pole (opposite attributes). The precondition to receive a soul is the existence of a Vessel, and a Vessel is the aim for the Creator.

Creation is eternal. Time and motion do not exist. We only speak of inner sensations of the creature. Changing inner situations evoke the sensation of time and motion. *The Zohar* speaks of spiritual degrees and of situations of the eternal soul, about measures of its fulfillment with the Light of the Creator. But the sensation of animate life can accompany a soul if a person receives it. Otherwise it is as it says: "...so that man hath no pre-eminence above a beast" (Ecclesiastes 3, 19).

DELIGHT AND PLEASURE

The purpose of creation is to delight His creatures. The complete Creator can only delight them with completeness. The Creator cannot create an incomplete creation. By "complete" we mean that only He fills the entire reality, which is why He is the only One. Because of that, we have a desire to be filled with Him. That desire is satisfied entirely, unreservedly. That is why His state is called *Ein Sof* (infinite).

But the Creator creates that situation for the creature to feel itself complete in its own right. For that to happen, the creature must attain a sensation of appreciation. We can only acquire that out of the sensation of the oppositeness of form and incompleteness. That is the purpose of us being distanced from the Creator to a state called "this world." Here, the creature feels corporeal animate pleasure - our current situation - instead of feeling the Creator.

The more we creatures become aware of our incomplete situation - which is possible only by studying Kabbalah - the more we become aware of the perfection that is the Creator. We begin to realize that perfection is adhesion with the Creator, equivalence with His attributes, being filled with Him.

During our studies, we realize that to be complete means to be as close as possible to the Creator, as similar as possible to His attributes, and to equalize with His form. As a matter of fact, that is already the situation, but we cannot feel it as such, and therefore we cannot regard it as such.

As we come to understand ourselves and the Creator, we begin to feel the completeness as though we are returning to it. Our sensation of fulfillment in these situations is called "pleasure," and the desire to feel the Creator as supreme completeness is called "Vessel."

THE FEELING OF COMPLETENESS

It is only possible to understand and appreciate completeness when one feels the Creator, because only He is perfect. Furthermore, the power to correct is also given by the Creator. Therefore, the purpose of the study, in the beginning, is to attain the sensation of the Creator. Then, everything becomes clear. Before that, we cannot understand what completeness is, and the Creator chooses to be shown to us precisely through our most incomplete attributes.

THE ACTIONS OF THE SCREEN

Spiritual objects are things that the Kabbalist creates over his or her screen. They are the result of the impact of the Light on the screen of the Kabbalist. As a result, a new picture of the spiritual world is created in the Kabbalist's mind. Spirituality is only born after a spiritual coupling, whose power determines the depth of the spiritual picture. If the Light does not hit the screen, nothing new is born, and all that a person gets is the picture of this world.

In other words, to beget a new spiritual object means to build from our substance (the desire) the image of the Creator, through the screen. In fact, the screen is a sculpturing tool in the hands of the Kabbalist. One observes him or her self from the side (restricts the desires, and erects a screen made of the intent not to receive for oneself). One uses the screen to cut off desires that one cannot simulate to the Creator (the "stony heart").

Kabbalists bring desires in which they can resemble the Creator to equivalence of form with the attributes of the Creator, to the extent that their screen can bear it. Thus, the higher the degree, the more one resembles the Creator. One studies the attributes of the Creator (the upper nine *Sefirot*) and then adopts them.

FROM THE CREATOR TO THE CREATURE

Here is what happens from above downward:

1. The four phases of Direct Light.
2. The birth of the world of *Ein Sof*.
3. The First Restriction of *Malchut*.
4. The birth of the world of *Adam Kadmon* (AK).
5. The Second Restriction.
6. The breaking of the vessels.
7. The creation of the worlds: *Atzilut, Beria, Yetzira, Assiya*.
8. The creation of the soul of *Adam ha Rishon* (the First Man).
9. The breaking of *Adam's* soul into pieces.
10. The descent of the pieces to our world.
11. The development of the souls by descending to our world, to our present state.

As you can see, the way down here is very long, but we can already come to certain conclusions about the nature of creation, the attributes of the Light and the Vessel.

MALCHUT AND THE WORLD OF EIN SOF

We must refrain from interpreting *Ein Sof* as a term of time or place. *Ein Sof* is something endless, unlimited by action or attributes—hence the name *Ein Sof* (lit. No End). Spirituality has no time or space. Therefore, these two limitations of our world do not apply to the spiritual world. For that reason we cannot imagine spirituality for what it is. We cannot imagine a cup that, although filled to the rim, is still in a state of endless filling (naturally, everything is measured according to the cup itself, because we measure everything with regard to the receiver).

Malchut, the soul, corrects itself through the worlds. The worlds are degrees of concealment or manifestation of Light. Time and again, the soul receives desires (which are the Vessels) and Light (the power to correct the desire) from the degrees.

By using that desire and the Light of correction, the soul, by correcting itself, seemingly rises to the same degree from which it received the power and desire to correct. All and all there are five worlds, within which there are five *Partzufim*, with five inner *Sefirot*. Together they make up 125 degrees. But there are still an enormous number of transitory situations.

Malchut is the tenth *Sefira*, the last one after the nine *Sefirot* of direct Light that extend from the Creator. *Malchut* receives the Light from all other nine *Sefirot* and divides in ten parts. Those ten parts of *Malchut* are the worlds and everything in them.

All nine other *Sefirot* before *Malchut* (also called the "Upper Nine") are attributes of the Light. *Malchut* must resemble those nine *Sefirot*. The extent of resemblance between *Malchut* and the nine *Sefirot*, which are the attributes of the Creator, depends on the power of the screen in *Malchut*. But the resemblance of *Malchut* to the nine *Sefirot* exists even with the smallest screen.

Therefore, even a minimal screen should make *Malchut* resemble all nine other *Sefirot*. Thus, any spiritual attainment is comprised of a whole picture (which includes all the *Sefirot*). A picture with a minimal screen can be made of a small number of shades or details, but it still makes offers a relative picture of all nine *Sefirot*. Just as, when we are born, we perceive with all five senses, regardless of whether we are adults or children, the power (depth) of our attainment depends on the power of our screens.

THE EVOLUTION OF MALCHUT

The term, "world," means concealment, hiding, limitation of the extension of the Light. But every situation of *Malchut*, of the collective soul, is also called a "world." The world of *Ein Sof* is a state of unbounded fulfillment of the soul. Everything that fills the soul is called "Light" or "Creator." But in order to be filled with the intent for the Creator, and thus equalize with Him, *Malchut*, the soul, gradually corrects the intent from *for me* to *for the Creator*. It empties itself in the first restriction, hides under five covers, worlds, and gradually, in accordance with the acquisition of the screen (the aim for the Creator).

Then, it exposes itself to the Light, the Creator, like a bride before her groom. Her degrees of correction, her exposure, her fulfillment with Light, are five worlds with five *Partzufim* in each world and five degrees in each *Partzuf*, all and all, 125 degrees.

It is also possible to divide the spiritual distance to 613 degrees (*Mitzvot*), or to 6,000 degrees – three groups of 2,000 in each. But the distance itself, the extent of the correction of *Malchut*, remains the same.

THE LIGHTS OF MALCHUT

Malchut (the soul) is divided into five parts (from fine to coarse): *Keter, Hochma, Bina, Zeir Anpin,* and *Malchut,* in ascending order of the power of the will to receive. The strongest desire takes the last part – *Malchut*. These desires receive five pleasures – Lights that fill them respectively: *Yechida, Haya, Neshama, Ruach, Nefesh.*

In the spiritual worlds there is a law called "the opposite value of Lights and Vessels": the coarser the desire that aspires to receive greater pleasures, the more Light it extends. But the Light goes not into the coarse desire, but into the finest one, into the desire to give without reward for self, because the Light and the finest desire to give are in equivalence of form.

It is also customary to say, "The Lights enter the *Partzuf* gradually." But any change in the Light means a change in the Vessel, and therefore, in the entire *Partzuf*. Everything is new each time, all five *Sefirot* and all five Lights.

SEFIROT

Sefirot are attributes that are given to the creature, the lower one, through which to feel the Upper One, the Creator. That is why the *Sefirot* express supremacy, the attributes of the Creator, attributes that the Creator wants the creatures to attain in order that they feel Him.

Just as we capture a person by his mind, which is his essence (whereas the body is only an outer clothing), so is spirituality grasped through its clothing, because the essence is in the interior attributes behind the clothing. Externality is only needed for the purpose of acquaintance, and not in and of itself.

A person attains the Creator through the *Sefirot*, meaning through His outer appearances. Similarly, we know others for certain only after we know all their attributes and reactions in varying situations. Through the *Sefirot* we will ultimately come to know reality, which is all a dressing for the Creator, just as the body is a dressing for the soul.

The Creator works within a person's soul. Therefore, those who learn to attain the Creator know Him and attain Him by His actions in their own souls, meaning by the action of the Light on their own points of *Malchut*.

Completeness is a pleasure that is sensed only after there is a hunger for something and a shortage of it, to the extent of the incompleteness that was felt prior to receiving delight.

It is impossible to sense continuous pleasure in this world, because nature has it that hunger and satisfaction do not come together. Precisely that attribute is given to the soul in order to feel hungry, in order to crave pleasure, so that one will learn that although one is able to satisfy the hunger, one will never get one's fill.

But the Creator wants to delight us, which is why He sends us a special fulfillment. The souls try not to spoil that satisfaction by crossing the line. It is only in this way that they arrive at completeness. The hunger and desire do not go away—on the contrary. As a result, the souls extend more fulfillment from a wholeness that does not fade, an eternal wholeness.

We know that we enjoy eating because of prior hunger, the sensation of craving. As the craving disappears, so does the pleasure. The Creator gave the souls a great "trick" that prevents them from being satiated, despite their receiving pleasure. The fuller they feel, the hungrier they grow. That is the perfection of the action of the Creator.

DIRECTIONS OF DEVELOPMENT

When we say that everything moves from up downward, from the root to *Malchut*, one may misunderstand that we are speaking in terms of an area, place, or distance. In the spiritual world, there is no volume or place. It is like describing our feelings: we say "deep emotion," "high note," "great joy," etc. Creation can be described as spreading from the Creator, from above downward; from the Upper One, from the exalted attributes, to the lower one, the lower attributes.

But we can also look at the development of creation from within, from the Creator outward to a point that draws farther from Him, like moving from the innermost, the most personal and hidden, to something external and less important. We can also speak about the development of creation as though the Creator surrounds it, "wrapping" it with His goal and controlling it from all sides. Creation is within, like an egg inside a brood hen.

There are other descriptions of just one thing: the relationship between the creation and the Creator. The actual words are merely tools that we use, depending on which attributes, characteristics, qualities, and interrelations we are talking about.

THE SPIRITUAL VESSEL

The Creator created a desire to delight, meaning a desire to feel pleasure. But when the desire to enjoy receives – it feels shame. That is why one cannot attain eternal delight by receiving, because receiving restricts the Light and even extinguishes it, thus nullifying itself.

For that reason, the only way to take pleasure is to enjoy not the pleasure itself, but the contact with the giver of the pleasure. If the pleasure of the giver is what you get from Him, then your pleasure will not disappear and will not diminish your desire for pleasure.

On the contrary! The more you receive, the more you give and enjoy. That process lasts indefinitely. However, the pleasure that we derive from sensing the one who gives is infinitely greater than the pleasure we receive when taking for ourselves. This is because the first kind of taking ties us with the Complete Giver, the Eternal One.

Thus, a mere desire to receive is not considered a Vessel yet, because it is unsuitable for reception. Only if there is a screen over the desire to enjoy (a screen is the intent for the Creator, meaning a willingness to take pleasure only to the extent that it delights the Upper One), does the desire become worthy of reception, and can then be called a "Vessel."

From this, we can understand that all we really have to do is acquire a screen! When the will to enjoy receives and feels the giver, it feels both pleasure and shame, because by receiving we become opposite to the Creator. The presence of the giver makes the receiver feel shame, and that shame stops us from enjoyment. When we receive, we feel we must give something back to the giver, to equalize with the giver so as not to feel as if we are only receiving.

The sensation of shame is also called "hell." There is nothing worse than the sensation of shame because it is the sensation of being totally opposite from the Creator. The Creator purposely paired receiving with shame. He could have avoided it, but the phenomenon of shame was created specifically for us so we could learn to receive from Him, to delight without shame.

That is why we, as creatures, (the will to enjoy) immediately felt ourselves to be receiving from the Creator and decided and acted out a restriction (limitation of the Light) on the receiving of the Light. That act is called the "First Restriction."

A giving Vessel is one that still cannot receive for the Creator, but can only refrain from receiving, because if it would receive, it would be for itself. The creature can exist without receiving Light because the sensation of shame extinguishes its pleasure at its reception, and turns the pleasure of reception into torment.

Then, when we feel the desire of the Creator to please us, we decide that despite the sensation of shame, we will accept the pleasure because that is what the Creator wants. Therefore, by doing so, we can bring pleasure to the Creator for His Sake, not for ourselves. The act remains as before, and we still receive, just as we did when we felt shame, but the intent of the reception has now changed.

The decision has been taken only out of the desire to delight the Creator, despite our sensation of shame. But we as creatures discover that by acting for the Creator, we do not feel ourselves as receivers, but as givers, equal to the Creator.

As creatures, through our equivalence of form with the Creator, we feel ourselves as the Creator: total wholeness, eternity, unending love and pleasure. But the decision to restrict the reception of Light (the First Restriction), to receive Light only with the aim for the Creator, will come only if we feel the Creator, the Giver, because only the sensation of the Creator can awaken such a resolution in us.

The question arises: if the presence of the Creator can evoke such a sensation in us, how can we say that the decision was really for the Creator? After all, the First Restriction was a consequence of the shame, and the reception of the Light was seemingly a result of the pressure of the Giver.

Therefore, in order to take an independent decision to receive for the Creator and in order to resemble He who created the creatures in order to delight them, the Creator has to be concealed, so that His Presence would not be compulsive, like placing a knife on one's neck. That is why there must be a situation where we creatures feel that we are the only ones here. Then, all the decisions will be our own.

THE LIGHT OF CORRECTION AND THE LIGHT OF FULFILLMENT

There is a Light that fills the desire to enjoy, meaning the Vessel, and there is a Light that corrects it. The latter is the Light that gives the Vessel the intent for the Creator and builds the screen over the desire. These two Lights act completely differently on the Vessel: the Light that corrects is called "the Light of correction of creation," while the Light that fills it is called "the Light of the purpose of creation."

The Light of correction can enter the Vessel even before there is a screen; it is specifically for the purpose of building a screen. It gives the creature a feeling that the Creator is supreme and mighty, and from that feeling the creature subdues its nature in order to draw near the Creator. That is how the Vessel acquires a screen. When one acquires the intent for the Creator, there is a *Zivug de Hakaa* (spiritual mating) and the Vessel is filled with Light.

TWO SCREENS

A Vessel is a desire that receives Light, the response from the Creator. It is the intent not to act for me, but for interests beyond my own. That is why we don't consider the mere desire to be a Vessel, but rather the screen, the altruistic aim to bestow, the returning Light.

The Light is the Creator. We always speak from the perspective of the Vessel, the creature. Any other perspective that is not from the sensation of the Vessel is unfounded. In the state of *Ein Sof*, after the Vessel receives the Light for itself (in order to receive), it decides never to do it again. It decides to restrict the reception of Light in its own desire to receive for itself.

That is called the "First Restriction." From that state down to this world, all the Vessels wish not to receive Light in order to receive. In other words, the law of the First Restriction is kept in all the degrees. The power to keep the restriction is called a "screen," because it protects the desire from using the Light for self-profit. But other than that, there is another screen–not just for maintaining the Restriction, but also for receiving the Light for the Creator.

SPIRITUALITY AND THE LOVE OF MAN

A true act of love is when I do something good for someone I love only because I want to delight that person, even without their knowing that I'm the one who did this good thing, and without looking to derive any pleasure from it. Love would be my only motivation to act.

A true act of altruism (love of man) is when one party does not know about the other party, whether or not the party is giving. Otherwise there is pleasure derived from it. If the Creator knows about a person's act, this is already a reward. But for true giving, there need not be any kind of reward, except the very act of giving.

we always speak from the perspective of a person with real feelings and not of abstract creatures. One must come to that sensation of genuine giving step by step, meaning one must attain the spiritual level of giving while in the meantime performing it only mechanically. But all the while, we should be aware that such existence is only mechanical, in the degree of this world, our temporary place.

BINA

In the spiritual world, there is no such term as reason (mind). The mind is in constant pursuit of pleasure for me. *Bina*, however, is the state where the soul wants nothing for itself, a state called *Hafetz Hesed* (Delighting in Mercy).

6,000 YEARS

The books of Kabbalah speak about 6,000 years, which are – in the language of the branches – 6,000 degrees that each soul must climb. They have nothing to do with a calendar that you hang on the wall.

Rav Baruch Ashlag compared birth and death in our world to the changing of one's clothing. That changing is gradual from generation to generation, each time in more developed bodies with more developed minds and desires. There is no connection between the degrees in the spiritual world and the changing of the bodies. For some creatures, a thousand years of life will not be enough for them to enter the spiritual world, while others complete their corrections within a single lifetime.

KABBALISTIC DEFINITION OF A JEW

Abraham, who went from Mesopotamia to the land of Israel, is called the first Hebrew (and the first Jew), because he was the first to cross from idolatry to the land of Israel (land - *Eretz* and Israel - from the words, *Yashar El*, meaning "directly to the Creator"). He went over from a state of worshiping idols to recognition of the existence of a Higher Power that controls everything, and identified himself with that power of his own free will. That is why he was designated Hebrew (*Ivri* - from the word Over) and Jew.

The terms "Jew" and "Gentile" are completely different in spirituality from the meanings we are familiar with. A Gentile is one who wants to unite with the Creator for his or her own pleasure, while a Jew is one who wants to do it in order to resemble the Creator (meaning become an altruist). The word Jew comes from the Hebrew word *Yehudi* – *Yechudi* (meaning unique and unified), because that person unites with the Creator. As you can see, it has nothing to do with genetics or the location from which you come.

SPIRITUAL DIVISIONS

Creation - a desire for pleasure - divided itself into the nine attributes that it received from Him: the upper nine *Sefirot*, and *Malchut*, the tenth *Sefira*. Thus, everything in reality is initially divided by ten. Then there are other divisions: a *Partzuf* divides to the three *Sefirot* of the *Rosh* (Head), and the seven *Sefirot* of the *Guf* (Body).

Then there is a division to twelve, which stems from the number of *Partzufim* (faces) in the world of *Atzilut*. In the wisdom of Kabbalah you will find the explanations for every division and the interrelations between them.

THE SEFIROT YESOD AND ZEIR ANPIN

Zeir Anpin has to be in contact with *Malchut*, in order to convey the Light to her. For that to happen, he must build a special *Sefira* to serve as a bridge between *Malchut* and him, meaning that it will possess similar attributes. For that purpose *Zeir Anpin* consists of:

1. *Hesed* – the *Keter* of *Zeir Anpin*
2. *Gevura* – *Hochma* of *Zeir Anpin*
3. *Tifferet* – *Bina* of *Zeir Anpin*
4. *Netzah* – *Zeir Anpin* of *Zeir Anpin*
5. *Hod* – *Malchut* of *Zeir Anpin*
6. *Yesod* – the sum total of all the previous *Sefirot* (like a salad made of five original components that when put together, form a new attribute).
7. After *Yesod* comes the collective *Malchut* – the creature, the soul, the part that must unite with the Creator (*Zeir Anpin*) through equivalence of form. *Malchut* is the creature and *Zeir Anpin* is the Creator. *Zeir Anpin* is the one to which all prayers to be raised and corrected turn, and he, at the request of *Malchut* (MAN), builds a bond with her – contact and coupling – through his *Sefira* of *Yesod*.

THE SOUL

The Zohar writes about the relationships between all five *Partzufim* of the world of *Atzilut*, which is the world that governs reality. It says: "Therefore shall a man leave his father and his mother" (Genesis 2, 24), meaning the soul will become independent from its mother and father, attain completeness and independent coupling with *Malchut*, to unite with the Creator, and create new *Partzufim* – corrected souls.

A soul is the *Partzuf* of *Malchut* of the world of *Atzilut*. *Zeir Anpin*, the Creator, is her husband. The *Partzuf* of *Abba ve Ima* – *Hochma* and *Bina* – provide the soul with everything she needs.

AN AWAKENING FROM BELOW

In the Kabbalah, everything is described from the perspective of the emotions of the attaining Kabbalist and the way the Creator is revealed to that person. Even when we speak of the Creator, and seemingly only about Him, regardless of ourselves, we still rely on our own understanding of Him.

Our desire for a spiritual ascent stems either from Above (the Creator), or below (from us). Of course, it is only the Light that rocks and awakens us, as Vessels. But then, either we clearly feel that the Creator is the one awakening us from Above, or we do not feel the influence of the Creator, but only the side effects of that influence: our inner will, meaning that there is suddenly an aspiration for the Creator because the Creator has secretly awakened us.

THE SPIRITUAL FORCE CALLED "MESSIAH"

The term, "Messiah," comes from the Hebrew word *Moshech* (lit. pulling). This refers to the pulling of people up from the ignominious worldliness to a higher level. The Messiah is a spiritual force, the Upper Light; the Upper Spiritual Force that descends to our world and corrects mankind, raising us to a higher level of consciousness. It is quite possible that along with it will also be certain leaders who will teach others to enter the spiritual world. But in principle, it is a spiritual force, not a flesh-and-blood personality.

CONFIDENCE

Confidence is the ability to endure, to be constantly nourished by the goal. The attainment of confidence depends only on the attainment of Surrounding Light. That Light is ready and waiting to fill the soul when it completes its correction. Therefore, now, when that Light shines upon the soul, it gives it the sensation of protection and confidence.

Only a direct and concrete feeling of the Creator gives a person confidence and the ability to endure all the degrees of correction. It is done by the Creator purposely so that we will not be able to overcome even the lightest spiritual obstacle by ourselves, but will need the Creator every step of the way.

In our world, we can exist without the sensation of the Creator. But in the spiritual realm, we cannot. The extent of the sensation of the Creator is the extent of the actual confidence of a person, and I would add, our ability to defend against disturbances.

WHO IS A FRIEND?

The word, "friend" (*Haver*), stems from the word, "connection" (*Hibur*), unification. The connection is only possible if there is a resemblance in attributes, thoughts and actions. Thus, according to the equivalence of attributes, a friend can be nearer or farther. Your "friend" (*Reacha*) stems from the root *Rea*, which means "near."

WHAT IS HUMBLENESS?

Humbleness is the most important trait. There is a special chapter in *The Zohar* called The Book of Humbleness (*Safra de Tzniuta*). Through the screen, we become like the Creator, precisely in the attribute of humbleness! This happens because we suppress our own nature and place the Creator above ourselves.

Humbleness demands of us to be aware of the lowness of our own nature, and to aspire to acquire the nature of the Creator – the attribute of giving, bestowing. Humbleness is the ability to activate our own nature to enjoy with the intent not for ourselves.

RIGHTEOUS AND EVIL

Any spiritual degree is divided in two parts: righteous and evil. If one justifies the Creator, that person is regarded as righteous, while one who condemns Him is regarded as evil.

A person who is in the world of *Assiya* is regarded as evil, but in the world of *Yetzira*, that person is regarded as evil and righteous. In the world of *Beria*, the same person is righteous. Before one enters the spiritual worlds, one does not fall into any of the above categories, because from a spiritual perspective, one does not exist.

RIGHTEOUSNESS

A righteous person is someone who has attained a spiritual degree called "righteous." This person has attained the screen that stands and prevents all pleasures from entering and filling the will to receive. That is why the righteous can always justify the Creator.

As for "the righteous that inherit the land," in each new degree, the righteous inherits, or receives new desires (desire – *Ratzon* – stems from the word land – *Eretz*) and places over them a new screen, called "receiving for the Creator."

GOOD AND BAD

The corporeal meaning of good and bad does not correspond to spiritual laws at all. It does not mean that it is opposite, that bad in our world is good in spirituality. That is not so! But it is true that our good deeds in our world do not promote us to spirituality.

I'm sure you've heard that the Creator is considered to be all goodness and benevolence, that He creates everything, and only good. So where is that good? What do we see around us? The answer is that the connection between this world and the spiritual worlds is nonexistent from below Upward. It can only be made from Above to below. Otherwise, everyone would willingly come to the Creator and would not need the correction from Above.

POWER OF LIGHT

Evil is lack of Light. It all depends on the intensity of the Light: when Light shines a little stronger, we feel it as good, as rest. That is the Light of which people speak who have experienced clinical death. A smaller amount of Light is sensed by us as states of depression, disaster and disease. It all depends on the power of illumination that shines over each person individually. "Bad" is actually the lack of Light.

PUNISHMENT?

There is no punishment in spirituality, only correction, which brings us to the attainment of perfection. In our present level of development, we normally picture a reward as receiving what we want. Therefore, the reward depends on the degree of each person's soul.

One must reach a state where the reward will be found in doing something for the Creator. Then the effort to add to the intent for the Creator is considered work that merits a reward. However, the work itself is actually the reward. Its cause - the will to receive - and the effect - the reward - become one. Time and pain vanish, to be replaced with a sensation of total completeness.

WHAT IS SIN?

First, let me stress that anything that happens in our world has no bearing on the Upper World, because one does not evoke any spiritual act by one's physical actions. When a person enters the Upper World, having acquired a screen, the person performs spiritual acts, using all of the 613 desires with the aim for the Creator, from the weakest desire, the first degree in the spiritual world, to the strongest, the highest desire of the spiritual world.

There are two types of pleasure:

1. The Light of Wisdom - felt in the desire for pleasure.
2. The Light of Mercy - felt in the desire to delight.

Both types can be received only with the intent for the Creator, not with the intent for me.

There are four actions that can be performed, depending on the measurement of the correction:

1. Receive pleasure for myself.
2. Give pleasure (delight) for myself.
3. Give pleasure (delight) for the Creator.
4. Receive pleasure for the Creator.

Ejaculation, in the Kabbalistic sense of the word, is an act of reception of pleasure, meaning Light of Wisdom, inside the uncorrected (lacking a screen) *Malchut*, while using the intent for me.

A correct use of the Light of Wisdom is attained only through a correct mating between the desire to give and the will to receive, between

Zeir Anpin and *Malchut* of *Atzilut*. The souls compel them to mate by raising a desire for correction, called *MAN*.

Only at the end of correction, when there is a screen over all the desires, will it be possible to receive without limits. That is why in the holiday of *Purim* there is a *Mitzva* to drink until you cannot tell between good and bad, because it symbolizes the End of Correction.

END OF THE WORLD

The end of the world refers to the end of the situation we are currently in, which is the worst and lowest of all. The end of that situation is considered a passage, after which a person begins to identify self with one's soul, to be in the spiritual world. That ends the question of whether to live in this body or outside of it. One stops feeling under the authority of one's own body, and that is called "the end of the world." From now on, one feels only the life of the soul.

HELL

Hell is the sensation of shame – the only sensation that the ego cannot tolerate whatsoever, because it humiliates it and completely revokes it. The sensation of hell places the creature in a lower status than the One and Only, the Creator, Who exists outside him. It shows us that we are the lowest and the meanest of entities. The ego cannot tolerate this to such an extent that it is willing to give up its own attribute. That is the reason that hell is felt precisely by those who are called "evil," meaning those who call themselves evil, because they want to become righteous and to justify the Creator's actions towards them.

PARADISE

Paradise is a perfect state, one that is attained after having finished correcting our will to receive and attaining complete adhesion with the Creator. Adhesion means equivalence of all one's attributes with those of the Creator, the attainment of complete awareness and the sensation of eternity and perfection. We are compelled to attain it, and we can do it in this very life.

HAPPINESS

Happiness is the sensation of the fulfillment of the internal capabilities of a person. It is fully clarified only when we realize precisely what and how we should fulfill, what our goal is, how eternal it is and independent, and to what extent it is the one meaningful thing in the world that is now being realized. In other words, happiness is the sensation of nearing the Creator, because that is the purpose of creation – a sensation of advancement toward a never-ending wholeness.

FEELING THE PASSAGE

A person goes through all the processes both before and after crossing the barrier, but the crossing itself is impossible to predict in advance. Crossing the barrier occurs only in a one-way direction, to the spiritual world but not back to ours. It means attaining *Lishma*, the intention for the sake of the Creator, and consequently, complete unity with Him, like a fetus inside its mother's womb, hence being filled with such a sensation, we certainly realize we are THERE.

THE TREE OF LIFE

The Tree of Life means the correction of altruistic desires (above the *Chazeh*) and working with egoistic desires (below the *Chazeh*) with the intention to give in the entire *Partzuf Adam*.

CHAPTER 10.
PERCEIVING THE SPIRITUAL

Our perception of the spiritual is actually a change in our senses. Even an insignificant change in our senses will significantly modify our perception of reality and our world. Everything we sense is called the Creation. Just as our sensations are subjective, the picture we build is also subjective.

As mentioned earlier in this book, scientists constantly try to expand the limits of our senses (with microscopes, telescopes, all kinds of sensors, and so on), but all these aids do not change the essence of our perceptions. It is as if we are imprisoned by our sensory organs. All the incoming information penetrates us through our five sensors: visual, auditory, tactual, gustatory and olfactory.

All information we receive in our senses undergoes some processing inside us, and is sensed and assessed following one algorithm: is it better or worse for us? From above, we are given the opportunity to create a sixth organ of sensation. Kabbalah teaches that the only thing created is the desire to have pleasure and delight. Our brains are aimed only at the development of this sensation, measuring it correctly. The brain is an auxiliary appliance, nothing more.

The result of studying Kabbalah correctly is a comprehensive and thorough experience of the true universe, as clear, and even clearer than our present perception of the world. The perception of both worlds gives us a full and comprehensive picture, including the highest force, the Creator who rules the entire universe. If we study it correctly, using authentic sources in a group of like-minded people and under the guidance of an authentic teacher, we can qualitatively modify our organs of sensation and discover the spiritual world and our Creator.

Our initial state is such that we do not understand or perceive that something is hidden from us. Yet if we begin to appreciate this fact during our studies, we have taken a step in the right direction. After awhile, we begin to sense a Higher Force that establishes contact with us, places us in different situations, and the causes and effects of those situations become clearer.

I begin to think, "This particular situation was sent to me by the Creator so that I could let it go" or "Perhaps in this situation, I should behave differently." This kind of analysis and self-criticism is exactly what transports us to the level of Humans. Now we have become more than a mere animal that walks on two legs. The benefit here is that when we start sensing the Creator, we are able to see which of our actions are useful to us and which are harmful.

When we know the causes and effects of any given action, we begin to know what will be useful to us. Knowing this, we naturally will not do something that brings us punishment, but would always do what brings rewards. So the revelation of the Creator brings us the chance to behave correctly in any situation and receive maximum benefit from that situation. Such a person is called a "righteous person." The righteous perceives the Creator, the reward for all good, as well as the additional reward for not violating a commandment.

A righteous person is one who justifies the Creator. Along our path, as we increasingly perform corrections, we receive more and more Light. That Inner Light is our perception of the Creator. With each new revelation of the Creator, we ascend the spiritual ladder one rung at a time. With our "spiritual feet" firmly on that rung, we then receive a new portion of Light.

We finally reach a level where the end result has absolutely nothing to do with us. It might be good or bad for us, but we still perform that spiritual commandment. When we have finally reached this level, we see the Creator as totally kind and every one of His actions as perfect. This all stems from reaching a certain degree of revelation of the Creator.

As we move along the 6,000 steps, we realize that everything the Creator does to us and to our fellow humans stems from the desire to endlessly delight all created beings. We are then overcome by a feeling of endless gratitude and a desire to thank the Creator.

All of our spiritual actions are aimed directly at giving to the Creator. In other words, we are doing more and more to please the Creator. This is called "the condition of eternal and endless love for the Creator." When we reach this stage, we understand that the Creator has only wished us good in the past.

In our current uncorrected state, this condition is virtually unknown. In fact, we blame the Creator for everything in sight, from being late to watch our children in a school play to the greatest tragedies of life. We tend blame the Creator for not getting what we wanted. It was the Creator that got us in trouble and brought us grief.

What we later discover is that the Light of the Almighty is consistent and unchanging, but when that Light enters an antagonistic desire, it arouses an antagonistic feeling in us. Spirituality is perceived on that edge between the positive and negative conditions we experience. The bottom line is, we should not fear any situation, even when it seems to be negative.

Often when we begin our studies in Kabbalah, we suddenly discover problems that were previously unknown to us. This is because we have accelerated the process of our spiritual growth. If we had not begun our studies, it would have taken us years to go through what we now go through in a few months, or even weeks.

If, during our studies and work with our friends, we listen correctly, meaning with the right intent, we will begin to be more and more "inside" what we hear and learn, and pay more attention to it. We will study the process of creation, the cascading of the spiritual worlds from Above to below, in order to draw in that spiritual Light described in the material we are studying. When we do this correctly, that Light will gradually cleanse our self-centered Vessels, correct them and convert them into altruistic Vessels.

When we study with others, often we will meet students who have been studying for years who are learning alongside a student who may have only started a few months ago. Yet both are able to advance without any hindrance in the least. It may come as a surprise that today's students come with a greater desire to understand everything. The reason for this is that their souls are more experienced, and are better prepared for the process.

Why do we study in a group? This enables us to utilize a very special means in Kabbalah. Studying the material with others of the same intent bonds us to the group's desire. This bonding allows us to humble ourselves with respect, creating an entirely different kind of acceleration. A person who studies within a group can actually reach spiritual levels after only a few hours, while it might have taken them years of study on their own.

So we actually have two ways to accelerate the attainment of our goal. First is the study of Kabbalah, which moves our efforts towards our goal from a subconscious process to a conscious process. Then, we have the group, which dramatically accelerates the conscious process. Using such a combined technique, we can spiritually advance literally thousands of times faster than we could by taking the unconscious route.

There are a few pitfalls to avoid. In today's times, Kabbalah has sometimes been corrupted into a fad, promising everything from a better sex-life to making more money. Of course, students will still receive some spiritual benefit for their efforts, but if the intent is not to reveal the Creator, but rather to gain some mundane benefit, they will be moving at a snail's pace.

There are also fanatics who actually do not have any clue as to the true purpose of Kabbalah. We call these people "pseudo-Kabbalists." For this reason, a new student should study only authentic literature and join a highly focused, single-minded group led by one teacher. Actually there are many stages one passes through before one ever discovers Kabbalah, but the last few stages involve a desperate search for the spiritual.

There have been times when a student wonders if it is acceptable to study other books or even look at different ideas claiming to be spiritual paths, and my response is the same. Kabbalists have always taught that "One should do exactly what the heart is leading them to do. For if other concepts of spirituality are on one's mind, they cannot even come close to the focus it will take to begin the study of Kabbalah in the proper manner. It is much better for a person to go and get it out of their system now, then after a few weeks, months or years, come back and work with a full and correct intent.

It is important to find authentic Kabbalistic sources whose content will induce thoughts about the Creator and the goal you need to reach. Then there is no doubt you will reach it. The sources that divert you from the true goal will not bring any good. The Surrounding Light, *Ohr Makif*, is drawn according to your desire. The Light will not shine if your desire does not aim at a genuine goal.

A prime example of this is none other than myself. I was first exposed to Kabbalah in my early twenties. I knew I was looking for something, but I was not exactly sure what that something was. I did study for a period, but then left and studied many other paths that claimed a quicker avenue to spirituality. It took many years for me to finally understand that Kabbalah is about only one thing—finding a form in which one can perceive the spiritual. The Hebrew term for this is *Hishtavut Tzura*, equivalence of form. It is precisely this goal that we must come to before we can seriously begin trying to reach the spiritual worlds.

You see, the spiritual world permeates our material world and shapes everything that exists in it. In other words, the roots of everything in our world lie in the spiritual world. By understanding those spiritual roots and our interaction with them, we can study our world correctly, allowing us to avoid making errors.

Most people are quite surprised when they first read *Talmud Eser Sefirot* (*The Study of the Ten Sefirot*) and find that the birth of the soul is incredibly similar to the conception of a human in the mother's womb, including the periods of pregnancy, birth and feeding. If the material were read like a novel, one might come to the conclusion that it is pure medicine. We then begin to grasp why we perceive such consequences of the spiritual laws of development in our world. The development of the soul is explained in a language that describes the development of the body in our world.

Horoscopes, astrology and predictions have nothing to do with Kabbalah. They are related to the body and its animal property to help us sense different things. Dogs and cats can also feel the approaching of some natural phenomena. In present times many people rush to use "New Age" techniques, trying to change themselves, their lives and their destinies. Destiny may be changed, in fact, if you exert an influence on your soul and learn how to control it. But again, this has nothing to do with the revelation of the Creator, which is about the desires within us and whom we intend to please through them.

There is another unique phenomenon when studying Kabbalah. As we become familiar with the laws of the spiritual world, we find that we can more easily understand the laws of our world. Sciences such as physics, chemistry, biology, etc., actually become simpler and clearer when examined from the viewpoint of Kabbalah. A Kabbalist dreams of rising above the present level, but not of descending. Kabbalists may perceive the roots of development of all sciences, if they wish.

Baal HaSulam, Rav Ashlag, sometimes wrote about the correlation between spiritual and material sciences. A great Kabbalist, the Vilna Gaon, enjoyed making comparisons between spiritual and material laws. He even wrote a book on geometry. Perceiving one of the highest spiritual worlds, he was able to draw a connection directly from there down to the science of our world.

As for those of us with no idea of the spiritual worlds, we shall read these books, pronounce the words, and try to understand their meaning. But even by just pronouncing these words with the right desire at heart, we are invisibly linking ourselves to the spiritual by attracting

Ohr Makif (Surrounding Light) from a certain level where the author was. When reading the books of the genuine Kabbalists, we allow the *Ohr Makif* to drive us forward.

The diversity of levels and types of Kabbalist souls account for the variety of styles expressed in Kabbalistic works, as well as the various degrees of Light intensity we may draw while studying them. However, the Light emanating from the various books of the Torah, including, from its special part, Kabbalah, always exists.

The Kabbalist Moses wrote a book about the wandering of his people in the desert. If we only take these writings literally as stories, then the Torah will have no impact on us. But if we delve deeper, and understand what is truly described there, the Five Books become a Kabbalistic revelation, wherein all the degrees of understanding of the spiritual worlds are expounded. This is exactly what Moses wanted to pass on.

The same relates to King Solomon's Song of Songs. Everything depends on how it is read and perceived. It can be taken just as a love song or as a spiritual revelation, which *The Zohar* describes as the highest connection to the Creator.

We constantly breed different desires, whatever they are. Our development depends on the level of these desires. In the beginning our desires are on the lowest level, the so-called animal desires. Later these are followed by desires for wealth, honor, social position, and so on. On a higher level are the desires for knowledge, music, art, culture, etc. Finally, we find the more elevated desire for spirituality. Such desires gradually appear in the souls after many incarnations in this world or, as we say, with the development of generations.

First the souls living exclusively in their animal nature life were incarnated in our world. The following generations of souls experienced desires for money, honor and power. Finally, these desires gave way to the desire for sciences and for something higher that the sciences cannot provide. To discover these desires is to discover the gateway to perceiving the spiritual.

CHAPTER 11.
INTENTION - OUR WORK

Our work begins with a search for the simple recognition of one singular truth. That truth is that there is no one else but Him. When we begin studying, we find ourselves drawn to many different and confusing elements of Kabbalah. We study many articles that approach Kabbalah from two very different directions. From one direction, Kabbalah is presented in a completely scientific and factual manner. From the second direction, Kabbalah is presented from a more emotional, "feeling" manner. Yet in the end, both directions lead to a single, fundamental conclusion: there is none else besides Him.

However, discovering this fundamental truth is no easy task, for it strikes at the very heart of our egos. In our research, we read about this truth and it makes perfect sense. Our minds have no trouble imagining that behind everything, yes, there is no one else but Him. But when we put our books down, or turn off the lesson from the computer and turn back to our daily lives, we encounter numerous situations that distract us from this principle.

The Kabbalah student reverts to the everyday working person with a wife or husband, a job, children, relatives, friends, hobbies, and all the problems that go with them. The lofty concepts learned in class or by reading suddenly fly out the window as the phone rings and a frustrated spouse begins to describe some minor catastrophe. The most profound wisdom seems to vanish into thin air as an angry boss marches into one's office complaining about some minor mistake.

As the months or even years pass, the student finds that he or she exists in some sort of war between the spiritual and the material. On one hand, every sentence written or taught by the teacher seems to bring new revelations. But the day-to-day acrobatics of dealing with life's problems, frustrations, and even joys seem to nullify the material.

This struggle marches merrily on until one day the Creator sends a thought that starts the process for the cure. What is that thought? It is the very essence of what the student began studying long ago, that there is none else but Him.

How does this thought manifest? It comes to us through a class, an article, or sometimes simple reflection, "Perhaps these obstacles that detain us are actually sent by Him." As the student delves into this concept, the desire to research, to test, to find out, arises. This is the start of a process that will lead us on an incredible journey of discovery.

One can compare this process to a judicial court. Our courts of law are set up with one sole purpose: to assign responsibility to someone. Their entire function is to assign blame for an overt action that has occurred. In smaller courts, there is simply a judge who delves into the facts of a certain matter and determines who is responsible. This is exactly what the Kabbalah student becomes—a judge.

What does the student judge? The student judges each and every disturbing action he or she perceives in order to determine who is responsible for that action. One assigns responsibility for these occurrences in one's life that seem to distract from the Creator. To whom does the student assign the blame for these annoying and sometimes devastating acts? There is none else besides Him; the judge lays the responsibility where the blame belongs, at the feet of the Creator.

Students learn it is the Creator Who sends obstacles to deter them from their path. But why would the Creator wish to deter them? Students work very hard, study sometimes well into the night, or early in the morning before work. They have attended many lectures and classes to hear their teacher explain these most profound writings. The student may even belong to a group that has chosen to study together. It seems that with all of this effort, the last thing the Creator would want to do is to try to dissuade His students, yet this is exactly what happens.

The student wonders, "How can I possibly advance?" and then learns that the Creator is providing him with the very solution to that problem. The problems, in fact, are the solution! The student finds that the problems are the very rungs of the ladder to climb up and advance toward the Creator.

At first, one is presented with small annoyances, distractions that remove one's attention from the Creator. But as the assignment of responsibility process begins, our judge finds that in the beginning, it is not that hard to bring the Creator right to the forefront. Yes, the Creator was behind this problem or that problem.

But as the student progresses, the assignments get harder. The obstacles grow stronger and stronger relative to the student's own strength and accomplishments. It seems that the more one is able to overcome, the harder the obstacles get. And one's assumptions are exactly correct. Sooner or later, the obstacles reach such a level that there is no way the student can make that most valued assignment of blame. Yet the Creator has provided a solution for this as well.

Let's go back to our example of the court to examine the Creator's solution. As previously stated, in a court of law, minor problems are handled only by a judge. But for major situations, the court inevitably selects a jury to help determine the assignment of responsibility. The judge actually nullifies himself or herself to the jury with respect to assigning blame and accepts their opinion without prejudice. In other words, regardless of the judge's personal opinion, one nullifies one's opinion and accepts the ruling of the group.

Now we see the true value of the student's group. Everyone in the group of Kabbalist students knows his or her responsibility to the group. That responsibility is to help any and all members in just this kind of circumstance. When that inevitable event occurs where the student simply does not have the power within to assign that responsibility to the Creator, the group steps in and reminds the student that "there is none else besides Him." The fortunate student once again realigns with his target, attaining the Creator, and progresses on toward the goal, that first moment of equivalence of form.

There is a law that rules nature and humankind harshly, and the Source of that law is a mighty Force called "the Creator." In difficult moments we turn to Him. But we sometimes feel that if we want to change something in our life, it means that we disagree with His actions, that we are not grateful to Him. So what is the actual cry of the soul, the one the Creator listens to and answers?

Unlike ordinary scientists, Kabbalists feel that which non-Kabbalists cannot, and having developed an extra sense, study the system of creation. But that power has an unchanging aim: to bring the entire system of creation to perfection. As a result, He acts on anything that is not in that state of perfection, and pushes it toward perfection. That process works equally on all parts of creation, and we feel it as pain and agony.

One can compare this to the pressure that parents put on their child out of the sheer desire for the happiness of their child. But while still growing and developing, the child feels their pressure as pain. As soon as the child attains the proper attributes, the pressure disappears and the child is happy and grateful.

From His perspective, everything in reality is already as perfect as can be. Yet, as long as we are not perfect, His Guidance cannot be felt as perfect. The Creator formed our initial corrupted situation deliberately, to give us a chance to choose perfection as something desirable and attain it by ourselves. How? Through the method called "the wisdom of Kabbalah."

Nature did not grant us the power to change ourselves. That is why we need not ask Him to change His Guidance, but to change us, so that we can feel His Perfect Guidance. The only form of progress that exists is in turning to the Upper Force for help. When we turn to this Force, we do not break His Law. On the contrary, we perform the one action we can perform.

But the cry must come out of a clear awareness of what it is we're asking for - is it for ourselves, to satisfy our desires in this world, or is it a cry for spiritual ascent? We now pray to Him because we feel bad, out of an egoistic motivation, and wish to feel good.

So do we condemn His Complete Guidance by that cry? Of course we do! But the question is, what does your heart feel? It doesn't matter if you cry or scream or stay silent. The Creator feels what's in the heart long before we do. When we ask to change ourselves not because we feel bad, but because we suffer from cursing the Creator in our hearts, that is already a request that is not self-oriented, for me, but is a true prayer for Him. To such a request the Creator responds at once!

We will certainly never ask the Creator for correction without feeling the need to do so. We see how people pray to God, asking for various things. But that is not the request for correction we speak of, not a prayer, as we understand it. A true prayer is a strong desire for correction of one's properties for reaching the Creator for His Sake.

We arrive at this kind of prayer very slowly, over years. First, we must cultivate it within ourselves. One first has the desires of this world, then for the Higher One, for the Creator, directed more and more towards the goal. In the process, we constantly change the definition of the Creator, the goal, and the correction.

Based on new understanding, one's prayer becomes oriented differently. As soon as one fully understands the goal, it is reached—the prayer bears fruit and one rises to the Creator. If one speaks from the heart, then every call to the Creator is new, even though the words are the same. Since the heart has changed, the prayer becomes so new that sometimes the same words seem strange to the supplicant.

We speak not about the Creator but of how we understand His Properties. Hence, our notions constantly change. By "our notions," it is meant that the ideas belonging to those who work on inner corrections and aspire to be like the Creator.

So what should one ask for? Ask for whatever you can ask, anything your mind will let you reach—and the Creator will give you everything, meaning everything that is needed for the attainment of the invocator.

One never knows how to act when seeking spiritual truth, but if one wants to grow spiritually, the Creator gives the seeker all that is necessary.

The feelings in our hearts are the prayer. But the most powerful prayer, as Baal HaSulam writes, is the feeling in one's heart during the study, the yearning to understand the material, meaning to match it with one's own properties. Obviously, what is really important here is the aim.

The aim is the one thing that the creature acquires in addition to the desire to delight in the Creator. The Creator made the creature with an inherent desire to delight in Him, in His Light. The creature feels only one thing: the absence or the presence of this pleasure. It doesn't even feel itself, but only pleasure and its quantity and quality.

The reason is that one can only feel oneself relative to something opposite the self. Therefore, the creature cannot develop from a sensation of pleasure alone. Such a feeling exists in the inanimate, the vegetative and the animate (including the animate human being).

The ability to sense the Creator is what differentiates humans from other forms of creation. It would be more correct to say that a person who feels the Creator is called "Man." In the language of the Kabbalah, Man is the Vessel that feels not only pleasure, but also the source of the pleasure. It is necessary to develop the will to this extent because the inanimate, the vegetative and the animate are different from one another only in the measure of their will to receive.

The measure of the desire causes changes in its quality. The will to receive (that is, beyond the inanimate) brings life with it. A greater will to enjoy creates animals and brings about movement in order to search for the pleasure, the feeling of the self as an individual entity.

Pleasure is possible only on the border between two opposing sensations. The sensation of oppositeness between creature and Creator creates the aim. A creature is a desire to enjoy. Only the aim allows for two situations: the aim for me, which is the corporeal state, and the aim for the Creator, which is the spiritual state, because in that one becomes similar to the Creator.

An aim for the Creator is the one thing we need to acquire from the Creator, the Light. That aim leads us to the purpose of creation and makes us equal to Him. Because of that, the Kabbalah is the "wisdom of the aim." And the aim is quite different from the act.

A physical act by itself does not make a difference in the Upper World! It is said that an act with no intent is like a body without a soul, and therefore it is regarded as a lifeless act, denied of the spiritual intent "for the Creator." But the aim comes gradually, according to one's progress in the study of Kabbalah.

The wisdom of Kabbalah is about intentions, and about how to turn one's heart to the Upper World. If a person begins studies and cannot add the right intent for the Creator, that time is called *Lo Lishma* (not for Her name), not for the Creator, meaning that at that time the student's actions are all for self.

But if a person does nothing to develop one's aims, then the person is not even working not for Her name, but is simply performing a lifeless act. However, the person should not stop doing it, because at some point the aim not for Her name will come, and *Lishma* (for Her name) will follow. Physical acts are always justified, but you have to aspire not to be limited by them.

A person cannot feel one's own heart or one's true situation. These are originally concealed from us and revealed only gradually, according to our ability to correct our original desires. It is very easy to open a book with prayers and read from it, but it is very difficult to attain the spiritual growth whereby the feelings in one's heart will match the written word; when the heart will recognize and live by the words as the veritable truth.

When we study Kabbalah, we extend illumination from the Upper Light. As a result, we begin to feel worse and our spirits drop. But we must understand that this is a state of correction; otherwise, we would not have been shown from Above that we are evil. We still don't feel ourselves as evil, and we are not in a state of the Recognition of Evil within us.

If we begin to study Kabbalah, we will see our true situation, which is characterized by the words "prayer is the work of the heart." This means that prayer involves working with the desires of the heart and correcting them. At that time we will begin to understand the true meaning of the words we are saying, and we will know what we have to do.

It will be clear that prayer is our work on the screen over our nature. Only the corrected heart, which feels its two extreme situations—the original condition when it was distanced from the Creator and its present one, when it is filled with the Creator —only such a heart can feel the blessing of the Creator and bless Him.

Your feelings during your studies—about yourself and the Creator— are your most honest prayer! That is what the Rav of Kotzk wrote in the book, *Yosher Divrey Emet* (Honesty and Words of Truth). That is why you do not need the proper prayer texts. The most correct thing is how you feel about the Creator.

Your understanding of the interpretation of the terms of Kabbalah will deepen according to the extent of the new feelings that will arise within you. For example, you will see that Pharaoh is the uncorrected characteristics of a person; that Exile is when one is distanced from the spiritual world; that Freedom is the liberation from the authority of your own nature, and so on.

You will be able to see that all the prayers in the prayer book and Psalms were written by people who went through those situations—Kabbalists in high spiritual degrees. That is why we, too, on our own spiritual levels, can use those prayers as a handy expression of our thoughts and desires.

But what about the mind? A prayer is the work of the heart, but the mind does not always agree with that sensation. For example, a person has to pass a very important and difficult test, and it terrifies him. His whole being may cry, "I don't want that test!" But his mind helps him understand how important it is to pass the test. Therefore, he turns to the Creator with a conscious request that he take the test and pass it.

The mind can help us decide whether or not to make the effort. We can influence it and convince it to obey us. Ultimately, we will make the effort and from Above we will be given new desires and emotions.

Feelings are what I experience in my will. The mind complements, corrects, evaluates and assesses the feelings, and that is why it can change one's attitude toward them. Therefore, all the things that affect the mind — friends, group and teacher — are what determine one's future. Kabbalah teaches us how to change the way we relate to our feelings so that "true" and "false" will have the power over us, instead of "bitter" and "sweet."

In Kabbalistic terms, a prayer is the request of the lower one for correction, and ascent of the desire to be corrected from the lower to the Upper *Partzuf* (raising MAN). If the lower one knows what to ask for, knows exactly what it wants, what it wants to be (meaning that inside there is already a sufficiently tormented desire, and only that desire), at that point the Upper One responds and the lower one is raised.

This process involves all the worlds, *Partzufim* and *Sefirot* from our world (the situation we are in right now) through the world of *Ein Sof* (infinity; the situation you cannot feel), although you are just as much in it as you are in our world. This is the total completeness, attainment and satisfaction.

The test and the proof that one has been answered by the Creator, has equalized with Him, and then has entered the spiritual world, is only in one's actual sensing of the Creator, of the Light, of equality and unity. That sensation is always intimate and personal, and is impossible to convey to a person who does not feel it. That is why the saying goes, "Taste and see that the Lord is good."

As long as one has not acquired a screen and has not felt the inner Light of the *Partzuf*, called *Taamim* (flavors), one thinks that one is not drawing away from one's nature, but rather falls deeper in to it.

Because the Light of the Creator influences one to a greater extent, one regards the remaining attributes (that are yet unchanged) as worse.

Thus, one thinks that it is not the Light that is stronger, but that he himself is changing for the worse. But while every step of the way seems to indicate one's situation is worsening, one who walks the road will see its end.

If I spot a negative quality in myself and suffer from the fact that it is in me, do I have to ask the Creator with all my might to help me correct it? Or is it better to try to ignore that characteristic because "one is where one's thoughts are," and think only of the greatness of the Creator, about how everything comes from Him, including that characteristic, and try to see His Guidance in everything. After all, He created me this way, so why should I correct myself?

The Creator created us opposite to Him in order for us to yearn to be like Him, precisely from that opposite situation. That is the purpose of all requests. Therefore, we should praise the Creator, knowing in our hearts that the attribute of the Creator is the most exalted and perfect.

But if all we do is cry about our misfortunes without forming any clear decision that we must be like the Creator, at least in some way, then our pleas are only for ourselves, regardless of the purpose of creation.

However, one cannot determine what one's requests of the Creator will be, or praise the Creator independently, because such requests are directly extended from within, from the heart, even before one knows their meaning. The desire, any desire, in one's heart is called "prayer." When one prays to be able to justify the Creator under any circumstances, that person is called *Tzadik*, meaning righteous, one who justifies the Creator.

Our effort is required so that the right attitude to the attributes and characteristics of the Creator will consciously and purposely formulate in us, so that we will want to cleave to the Creator. We are not the Creator, and cannot change anything within us. All we can do is prepare ourselves to want to change. That is the prayer.

Everything begins in the Upper World and then comes down to ours. Our mechanical movements (as well as all that happens in nature) have no effect on the Upper World, because our world is merely a consequence of it, meaning it follows the commandments of the Guidance that comes from Above.

Anything that happens here in this world is a consequence of forces, commandments and influences that descend from Above. The only things that rise from our world to the Upper One are the desires that come from the bottom of our hearts. Only they evoke responses in the Upper World. That is how they influence it. As a result, they also influence what comes down to us. The desires of a person from the bottom of the heart are called "prayer."

All our desires, without exception, are divided according to their aim into desires for myself and desires for the Creator. The Creator determines our desires and we cannot change them, because the Creator wants us to correct them. When speaking about the correction of desires, the idea is not to change the desire itself, or to suppress it, but to change the initial aim from for me into the desired aim, for the Creator.

The Superior Management exists for that sole purpose – to constantly fuel us with desires so we can slowly digest them and come to realize that they need to be corrected. All spiritual acts are actually corrections of the intent of our desires. In order to delight in the Creator, in His Light, we should change our aim from for me (in order to receive) to for the Creator (in order to bestow).

It is very difficult to maintain thoughts about the Creator. You may feel as though nothing is happening, or that your situation isn't changing. But in reality, if time passes, you have gone through something, because at any given moment there are changes in you. When the aim is to overcome some part of your preliminary desire to enjoy for yourself and correct its use, it can only do you good to be immersed in thoughts about the Creator.

You are reminded of the Creator to the extent that you make inner observations, although they are still not in your consciousness. You can speed up the process only through intensity of thought, by reading the essays of Rav Baruch Ashlag and the writings of Baal HaSulam.

Intensity of thought and power of thought are actually determined by the time you are connected in your thoughts with the object of your contemplation. You acquire that by practice, by trying to keep your thoughts impregnable despite disturbances. You must go through all of this yourself, as there is none as wise as the experienced. Kabbalah is a practical method that a person must experience oneself.

CHAPTER 12.
CONCLUSIONS

All sacred scriptures describe the feelings that we are expected to live out. The message is always the same: that we are to prefer spirituality to the lures of the material world, and to praise the Creator. The Creator does not need our praises, because He is totally devoid of egoism.

The only thing He wishes is to fill each one of us with delight. This is proportionate to our desire to choose Him amongst all other things, and to our aspirations to achieve attributes similar to His. The glorification of the Creator is an indication of the correct orientation of the *Kli*. The delights from bonding with the Creator can become infinite, eternal, and perfect and are only restricted by the intervening of a person's ego.

Altruism is a specific attribute, a means of correcting the *Kli*. Egoism does not bring anything good or worthwhile. It is obvious that the more people have, the more likely they are to be dissatisfied. The most developed countries often have an alarming rate of suicides amongst young and old.

One may give everything to a person, but this often results in the recipient's lack of appreciation for the simple tastes of life. Taste is sensed only when suffering and pleasure comes into contact. The fulfillment of a pleasure leads to the quenching of the desire to receive it. The Creator's commandment to change the egoistic nature of the *Kli* into an altruistic one is given for our benefit, not for His Sake.

Our present condition is called *Olam Hazeh* (This World), but our next condition is *Olam Haba* (World to Come). This World is what one feels at the present moment. The next elevated, perceived feeling leads to one's perception of the World to Come.

Even if every student attended a short course in Kabbalah and then walked away, those students would still receive something that would keep on living inside them. Each of us knows deep within us what is the most important thing in life. People are all different. Some were born smarter and are quicker, achieving success in business and in society. Often, they become wealthy and may begin to exploit others.

Others are born lazy, they grow and develop slowly. They are not very lucky. Some might even work harder than their smarter neighbors, but get little in return. We cannot assess each other's efforts in this world, as they depend on a great number of inner qualities that we are born with. There are no devices that could measure the inner, moral efforts of an individual, nor the physical ones.

Baal HaSulam, Rav Y. Ashlag, writes that approximately ten percent of the people in this world are so-called altruists. These are people who receive delight from giving. Just as an egoist may kill for not receiving, an "altruist" may kill for not being able to give. Giving is just a means of receiving delight for that person.

Such people are, in a way, egoists as well, because their intention is to receive something as a result of their bestowal. Naturally, they, too, have to undergo correction.

With regards to the spiritual, they are all the same. They must go a long way in order to grasp the inherent evil in their not being genuine altruists. This is the period in which they realize they are egoists. The coarser and more egoistic an individual, the closer that person will be to seizing the opportunity to move on to spirituality. In this case, egoism is as mature as it is enormous.

Now, one further step is required: to realize that this egoism is evil to us. We must then plead with the Creator to change our intention from receiving for our own sake to receiving for the sake of the Creator.

The attribute of shame appears in *Malchut* of the *Ein Sof*, when it realizes what *Keter, Behina Shoresh* is like. It is the sensation of the sharp contrast existing between the Light and itself. *Malchut* itself does not perceive the Light, only the attributes and properties which are awakened in it by the Light.

The Light itself does not possess any attributes. Whatever attributes *Malchut* feels are the result of the influence that the Light has upon it. All the reactions of the human organism are useful and necessary, whether we speak about the spiritual or material organism.

Our egoism is very clever. If there are any desires impossible to satisfy, it suppresses them in order not to bring needless suffering. However, the moment certain conditions arise, these desires resurface. The above is true for even a weak, ill or old person, who does not have any special desires except one: to remain alive. The organism suppresses the desires that are not to be fulfilled.

The evolution of the world is divided into the four stages of *Ohr Yashar*, when *Behina Aleph* turned to *Bet*, *Bet* to *Gimel* and so on. But when *Malchut* of the *Ein Sof* was formed, it absorbed all the desires of the upper *Sefirot*, which live in *Malchut* and do not change in any way. The fact that other worlds were formed later on does not bear witness to changing desires, but to evolving intentions.

Depending on the intention, different desires are activated. But the desires themselves do not change. Nothing new that was not there previously is created. It is the same with the thoughts that came to us today, but not yesterday. They were there before, but yesterday they were concealed from us. Everything is in a latent state inside of us, and there is a time for the unfolding of each action. Nothing new is created.

It is impossible to transform two different things into one another. For example it is impossible to change inorganic nature into organic, or beings of the vegetative kingdom into members of the animal one, and so on.

Intermediate classes do exist. For example, halfway between the vegetative and animal worlds are the corals. Between vegetative and animal there is an animal called "The Dog of the Field," which feeds on the soil. The ape is located halfway between the animal and human realm of existence. It cannot be simply an animal, but neither will it ever be a human being.

The only transformation that may occur is when a divine spark draws one to the spiritual and fosters the desire to attain, to reach for something higher. At this stage then, this two-legged creature becomes a true Man. There are very few people that may be called "Man" from the Kabbalistic point of view.

The development of science and technology is bound to reach an eventual deadlock and make us come to conclude that such is not the main goal. But first of all this state of deadlock needs to be reached.

Kabbalists have always organized groups of students. Under no circumstances are the students to be ranked or distinguished according to their desire to study. People are created with certain desires beforehand, and nobody knows why one is created that way and why another's desires are displayed in a different way.

Before a permanent group is formed, ranking and selection take place. Nobody, except for Chaim Vital, understood the Ari properly. The Ari, Rav Isaac Luria, lived in the mid 16th century and taught in Safed.

It is known that Chaim Vital undertook to study by following the new method worked out by the Ari. There were already great Kabbalists in the group of the Ari, but he nevertheless transmitted everything to Chaim Vital exclusively. The way a master in Kabbalah teaches depends on the type of souls that descend to this world.

Prior to the Ari, there were other systems and methods of teaching. Following the disclosure of the Ari's methods, it is possible for everybody to study; only a genuine desire is required. Baal HaSulam, Rav Yehuda Ashlag, did not modify the system of the Ari, he only extended it. He gave more detailed commentaries on the books of the Ari and *The Zohar*.

This is how those in our generation who want to study Kabbalah and draw closer to the spiritual realm may understand the inner essence of the studied material, and may establish analogies when reading the Bible (The Five Books of Moses, the Prophets and the Scriptures).

The souls that entered this world prior to the Ari perceived the spiritual as purely extrinsic. After the Ari's death, souls began to descend, and they studied and analyzed themselves and the spiritual world by means of a spiritual and scientific method. This is why the books issued before the Ari, are written as a narrative.

The books subsequent to the Ari's teaching, e.g. *The Study of the Ten Sefirot*, were written using terms such as *Behinot, Partzufim, Sefirot,* and *Olamot*. It is a psychological engineering, a scientific approach to the soul.

Each science possesses its own language. If the Kabbalist is not a scientist he or she will not be able to describe different phenomena using the required scientific terminology. The Kabbalist perceives the true laws of the universe, which are the foundation of the material and spiritual essence of all things.

In what language might one write the correlation between two objects? And what are the relationships between spiritual objects? How can one describe the spiritual force that holds this entire world together?

No specific formula in this world can convey all this. In the spiritual world, the Kabbalist may be able to pass on all his perceptions. But how can these perceptions be made available to the layman? Even if it were possible to somehow narrate them, nothing could be applied to our world until one has changed one's egoistic nature.

If people could modify their attributes to a higher level, they would be able to communicate amongst themselves in a spiritual language and perform spiritual deeds. One receives and suffers according to the level on which one stands. To rise to a spiritual level, a screen (*Masach*) is required, which is no easy task.

We are trapped inside a vicious circle from which we cannot escape. We thus ignore what is beyond that circle. This is why Kabbalah is called a "secret science," for those who do not know about its workings.

In his Introduction to the Book of *The Zohar*, the Kabbalist Baal HaSulam talks about the four degrees of knowledge: (i) substance, (ii) form clothed in substance, (iii) abstract form and (iv) essence. Science may only study substance and form clothed in substance. Form without substance is a purely abstract conception and does not lend itself to accurate analysis. The last, essence, which animates objects and triggers reactions, is unknowable.

The same applies to the spiritual world. Even a great Kabbalist may, while studying something spiritual, perceive substance and its makeup, in whichever form, though never the form without a substance.

Finally, when Kabbalists reach a certain required level, they receive a gift from Above: the disclosure of the secrets of the Universe.

DETAILED TABLE OF CONTENTS